Doing the Charleston: My Personal History of Scholarly Communication

T0348850

Doing the Charleston

MY PERSONAL HISTORY OF
SCHOLARLY COMMUNICATION

Katina Strauch
with Darrell W. Gunter

Against the Grain Media
Sullivan's Island, SC

Published in the United States of America by
ATG LLC (Media)

Manufactured in the United States of America
DOI: http://doi.org/10.3998/mpub.14621062
ISBN 978-1-941269-61-9 (paper)
ISBN 978-1-941269-62-6 (open access)
http://against-the-grain.com

Further materials related to the theme of this book can be found on the
Fulcrum platform at the following link: http://doi.org/10.3998/mpub.14621062

To Liz Weiss, especially, for her expert editing and suggestions! And to Leah Hinds for her eagle eye, steadfast patience, and good humor. Plus, I can't possibly leave out the ATG and Charleston Conference teams who made and continue to make the Charleston Conference and ATG possible!
My best love always!

CONTENTS

"Choose a job you love, and you will never have to work a day in your life." –Judy Romano

PREFACE

This is the story of the emergence of libraries and scholarly publishers on the scholarly communications scene in the 1980s and '90s, and the twenty-first century. Since I am the primary character, yes, some of it may seem like my story, but it is also about some of the bumps and hurdles we encountered. I am proud to be a librarian through and through!

PLEASE NOTE: Several names in this memoir have been changed for confidentiality.

Part 1

1973–1990: Old Problems, New Solutions

Chapter 1

FIRST STEPS

North Carolina

My uncle (my mother's brother) was an ob-gyn, and since I wanted to switch to an IUD, he assured me that, if I stopped the birth control pill for several months, I would not get pregnant. Anyway, he was wrong. In 1973 I got pregnant, and my glorious son Raymond was born. My husband was busy reading French history, so my wonderfully awesome mother came to help us keep Raymond off and on, until I made other arrangements.

In 1975 I enrolled in the University of North Carolina at Chapel Hill School of Library Science. My husband was busy trying to get his masters in French history at the same time. Academe was even more cutthroat back then than it is now, and my husband was not the exemplary student like some of his colleagues. I was in a hurry to get my masters completed and get a real job. My husband planned to go for the PhD, which would take several more years. He also wasn't in any hurry. That's the main reason we parted ways.

I was in library school, but there was one big hurdle: the administrator at the library school said that since I had a full-time job (I was the assistant library technician at the geology library) I could only take two courses at a time, which I balked at. It would take too long for me to finish my degree. I appealed to the dean of the library school (who I think liked me), and I was able to take three courses at the same time. Hooray! I remember what a great librarian friend Carolyn Lipscomb was. She was the map librarian at the geology library. She married Joe Lipscomb, an economist, and they had a son. We stayed in touch for many years!

I decided to part ways with my husband. At this point in my career, I didn't have a clear idea of where I was really going. I wondered if I should consider law school, but never completed the application. Looking back on it all, whew! I would have been a horrible lawyer. I didn't like combat, and I wasn't all that into studying law books. Both of my brothers became successful lawyers! Better they than I.

But about that time, my father invited me to travel with him to the Federal Reserve Bank of Baltimore, where he was considering taking a job. He introduced me to Liz Angle, a research librarian, whom he admired, and I bonded with her immediately. I did not want to be a librarian, but I decided not to abandon library school just then and began to study more earnestly.

Fresh out of library school with a masters in library science in 1975, barely thirty, I had been hired as the nursing librarian at the prestigious Duke University, a plum of a job for a new library school graduate. Duke was famous for its medical school, basketball teams, academic excellence, and Gothic architecture.

It was now 1977, and I had my masters in library science and a new proposal of marriage from Bruce Strauch, an old friend from college days. We decided to leave our beloved Chapel Hill. Bruce had graduated from law school and had located a temporary job in Winston Salem, NC. But we had set our sights on Charleston, SC, to find employment.

Charleston

Charleston, in contrast to Durham, NC, was a small town—shabby, mysterious, a place of antique buildings and walled gardens, palmettos, roots of ancient oaks lifting the sidewalks, banana plants, and jasmine—an absolute magic kingdom by the sea.

In August it rained every day, like a rainy season in the tropics, with a burning sun coming out afterward and turning the wet to steam.

Bruce found a law-teaching job at the Citadel, the Military College of South Carolina. I remember it was very military. There was some sort of military type who decided who would get a house or apartment on campus, and which house or apartment exactly. We moved into a great apartment and lived on the campus in faculty housing for forty years. It was probably the last place to keep such housing in the country, but has now abandoned that wonderful campus community life.

The Citadel campus was a self-contained village with its own police force, infirmary, doctors and nurses, cafeteria, library, bookstore, barber shop, gas station, playing fields—you name it. The campus was very formal and military. Faculty wives would wear formal dress for major cadet dances and events. I briefly interviewed for a job in the Citadel library, but the director said I would want time off when my husband was off, so he couldn't give a job to me.

Instead, I found an assistant head librarian job at a local technical school, which was up and coming, except for the bats sitting on the shelves at night. I had to work two nights a week in a rather rundown, old area of Charleston. There were cockroaches and bedbugs all over the place. Majestic Duke seemed far away. However, there were wonderful students, professors, and colleagues willing to help. The head librarian was very eccentric and promoted me over a male librarian who had been there longer.

I was still looking for more of an academic job, so I worked off and on for the South Carolina Low Country Area Health Education Center temporarily.

I went on an earnest job search once again. I had been certified as a medical librarian at Duke. But since there were no medical library jobs in Charleston at the time, that was irrelevant.

Hold your horses! We'd been in Charleston a couple of years, when a job opening appeared for an acquisitions librarian at a small college library downtown. I held my breath and put in my application. I had met Anne Kabler, the associate director at the Medical University of South Carolina (MUSC) Library, and her boss, Buzz Sawyer. Anne is easy to know, warm and friendly. It turned out that Buzz was friendly with Ellis Hodgin, my boss at the College of Charleston until he resigned. Small world. It also turned out that I had worked briefly with Mary Hodgin, who was in charge of interlibrary loan at the MUSC Library.

And guess what? It's easy to get a job with no experience when you are the only applicant!

I was ecstatic to get the job, in 1979, as the very first acquisitions librarian at the College of Charleston!

My First Day

The College of Charleston was small, barely five hundred students and a handful of buildings, but what an idyllic place: two quads and a cistern, a porter's lodge, huge live oaks, and flowering plants.

It was one of the oldest colleges in the country, founded in 1770, a land grant college long before Abe Lincoln passed the Land Grant College Act. Three of the founders were signers of the Declaration of Independence.

When I started working there, the state legislature had given the college a plot of ground below Calhoun Street (Boundary and Manigault then). The college was to sell lots and use the money for a building of their own.

Randolph Hall is now administration, but for ages it was the sole classroom, with labs—everything—along with the Towell Library.

In 1773, two sons of Charleston gentry on a grand tour of Europe saw the British Museum and decided America needed one. The first museum in our country's history was in the College of Charleston's Randolph Hall. Sea captains gifted all manner of curios. A whale skeleton hung from a ceiling.

On my very first day at the college, I remember walking amid all the colorful spring flowers and listening to mockingbirds, robins, and cardinals as I made my way to the Robert Scott Small Library for my new job. It was to inspire me to write a walking guide to the college, *Azaleas and Stucco* (Sandlapper, 1989).

Seems perfect, right? I thought so too.

The college infrastructure was small—the president, an academic vice president, and his secretary. The library staff was a library director and ten professional and paraprofessional staff members. The personnel director was an Army retiree. He was charming, but he wrote my social security number down wrong. Oops!

After I completed the paperwork, I walked to the library, where I met the library staff and my boss, the head of technical services. I was given a desk (not an office) in the technical services area, next to two cataloging librarians, a serials librarian, and three reference librarians, all of whom had offices. There was also a special collections librarian on the upper floor with all the rare and gift books.

Trouble Getting Along

I was shocked when, at the beginning of my second idyllic month, the head of public services librarian told me that the staff was trying to get the library director who had hired me fired! She asked me to sign a letter to that effect! She was very earnest. She talked about how she loved the college and the staff, but she had become disillusioned. She had compiled a thick notebook of some of the indiscretions of the director, many of which included being inebriated at college parties and having affairs with faculty wives. I decided that "discretion is the better part of valor."

Whew! Try to Stick to the Work Ethic

The library's professional staff was very young and naive, just like I was, so there was a lot of stress among them; there was jockeying for the best position in the hierarchy, the best office, best salary, best IBM Selectric typewriter.

I was so happy to take the job that I had overlooked the fact that to get my professional position approved, the director of libraries had eliminated the Library Technical Assistant V position and upgraded it to my professional librarian position. Oops. Imagine the possible resentment. Most of my LTAs, however, had not reached the LTA III level, and the highest ranking of my LTAs, the amazingly smart and capable Shirley Davidson, stayed on and was extremely supportive of me and the Charleston Conference! She is the Charleston Conference historian.

As I was learning about the duties of my new professional librarian position, the struggle to remove the director of libraries continued. There were high-level meetings with members of the library staff and the college administration. The professional staff was divided by public services and technical services staff. The head of technical services was on the director's side, and the head of public services was strongly against him. There were private backroom meetings that I was not always privy to.

My impression was that the library director was generally well-liked. He was attractive, and his wife was a great cook. Together they had two precious children. They had parties for the campus and the staff on holidays. He seemed to be respected by his peers. But several of the senior librarians had kept detailed notes about his missteps, and in the end he was encouraged to resign.

Search Committee

A search committee was set up to help find a replacement for the director. I was chosen as one of the members of the search committee. I was apprehensive. I had never been on a search committee before. This committee consisted of several professors with experience, the assistant to the academic vice president, and three senior librarians.

The director had been working with a committee of faculty members who I had met, and there was a small budget which had been apportioned among the academic departments. So, a year after I had taken the job in the library, I found myself chosen as one of the members of the search committee to replace him.

Our library staff continued to function as we always had, even though there was no director. I decided to survey the professional staff for their opinions and preferences. The provost had given the library a small budget to acquire new books.

I decided to assign subject selection areas to various librarians based on their interests and preferences. Most of the librarians were interested in the humanities subject areas; though I had no science background, I took all the science subject areas—biology, chemistry, physics, and mathematics. Many of these faculty members are still good friends.

Acting Director and Disagreement

An acting director, Dr. Stan Ralph, was selected right away and was to continue until a permanent director was hired. Stan was the person who had much visibility, plus the academic vice president was a fan of his.

There was considerable division between and among the favored applicants for the permanent director of libraries. Stan was the in-house candidate.

It was my first time grappling with questions about the role of a library director: Should library directors be hired based on proven innovative ability in librarianship, or based on a PhD in an academic subject? Should directors be obliged to fundraise, pioneer, create, and launch, or write articles on the White Whale?

In the final analysis, a director from "off" was chosen, not Stan. The new library director, Sheila, was a female, from out of town. She did not have a PhD; she was writing her dissertation on an unknown author whom no one knew about or admired. The group that had arranged the ouster of the former director preferred Stan. The provost assigned someone to assist Sheila in finishing her doctorate. Turned out that she had a relative on the College Board of Directors. Case closed.

I had done my best to stay neutral, though after Stan left the college, he frequently asked me for a reference.

The head of technical services was my boss, and I continued to be her friend. She loved horse racing, and we always picked favorites for the Triple Crown. I do remember getting a phone call from a colleague in Guam. Turns out that Stan had accepted the dean of libraries position on the island. She was at the airport to pick him up, and he didn't appear! Gosh! When I asked him about it, he called her to apologize.

Chapter 2

THE FIRST CHARLESTON CONFERENCE (1980)

My position was academic, tenure-track, which was a developing concept, meaning that I had to get involved professionally in local and national venues.

Enter an enterprising local scientist colleague, Matt Dominick, who was attempting to begin a small book fair for collectors of rare books to market and publicize their items. Matt had his own small bookshop and several local contacts. Matt's bookshop was in an old dilapidated building on King Street that also was a shoe repair place. I asked Matt if he thought maybe eventually we could turn the bookfair into a small meeting where collectors and librarians could have discussions about rare book pricing.

I had been at the college barely a year and a half and was trying to "cover my bases" and keep my job. Over the last few years, I had tried to keep in touch with librarians whom I had met. I was teaching a course on buying books for libraries for the College Center for Continuing Education. I also had meetings with my small staff to discuss book ordering. Relations with teaching faculty were progressing. I always liked doing different things, and a book fair sounded interesting.

The newly hired professional development dean at the college, Andrea Cusp, was recruiting faculty members to begin and teach new professional development courses. So I put in a proposal to teach a class about purchasing books. Since I had taught nursing students about library resources and had a book under contract because of a poster I had given, I offered to talk about book buying and selling to accompany the antiquarian book fair.

Matt welcomed my involvement!

Thinking Outside the Box

Amazingly, this was all approved in February, and I was assigned a venue near where the rare book dealers would be positioned.

The very first Charleston Conference was born.

Most meetings had separate sessions for publishers, vendors, and librarians, and I thought that was unfortunate, since we all had similar and interconnected problems and issues that were best solved if we talked together. (To paraphrase Karen Hitchcock-Mort, as she would put it at the opening of the conference, "the fiscal problem of the eighties was one of monetary limitation after years of relative plenty." We had to learn to tighten our belts!)

So, at the back of my head, I entertained preliminary thoughts of a blended meeting with publishers, vendors, librarians, et al., together. But right now, there was a lot to do, because the book fair was supposed to open in several months, and the proposal had just been accepted. Matt and I arranged to have bookshelves moved from his shop or constructed. We also started publicizing locally.

My colleagues were supportive. Matt was put in charge of recruiting rare and antique bookdealers to be exhibitors. We were able to locate thirty or so rare book exhibitors. I was amazed at the interest and learned a lot about rare bookselling. Rare and antique booksellers were fiercely independent and unique in their passion to locate the best item of their dreams. They weren't as into profitability as they were into discoverability.

First Conference Speakers

There were a lot of publishers and librarians who were interested in discussing what was happening, including exhibitors at the antiquarian book fair.

That first year, we had twenty-five participants and four well-known and famous speakers. I especially remember Bill Schenck who was at UNC-Chapel Hill (later the Library of Congress), and John Ryland who was at Hampden Sydney College. They both recommended I invite Paul Koda, rare books librarian at UNC-Chapel Hill, and Jake Chernofsky, publisher and editor since 1975 of *AB Bookman's Weekly*, a book trade publication of R. R. Bowker. He served on the National Advisory Board of the Library of Congress's Center for the Book. He also chose to publish the papers from the very first Charleston (Book Fair) Conference. We met in a small room in the Rivers Dormitory at the College of Charleston.

Next Move

Since the book fair had ended successfully, I was thinking about the next year, and if we should have another conference or book fair, since there was a lot of interest. The planning was sporadic. It has always been organic, natural, and not dependent on human actions! We did not have a committee or a group to recommend a program. We just talked to the people who had expressed interest in a future meeting, people like Bill Schenck from UNC-CH, Bob Barrows from Arno Press who had attended the first meeting, librarians Karen Hitchcock-Mort and Corrie Marsh who had also attended the book fair. We also spoke with Mike Markwith who was at Blackwells, Tom Leonhardt from Duke, and Nancy Rogers from EBSCO.

Changing Focus and Interest

Since I had spoken to many of the exhibitors and book-sellers, I realized that while we shared many of the core interests that we were passionate about, they had been trained differently than we had been. We decided that for continuing conferences, we should focus on the acquisition of all categories of scholarly books, and dubbed the conference, "Issues in Book and Serial Acquisition." I decided to barrel ahead with a meeting for librarians, scholarly publishers, vendors of books, journals, and booksellers. Interest had been expressed by all of these groups, since there was no alternative gathering. I had a small group of attendees and friends and volunteers who expressed a willingness to assist in planning and development. And the rest is history!

Chapter 3

THE CHARLESTON CONFERENCE
IN ITS EARLY YEARS

It was 1979 and I was thirty-three years old. I had a new tenure-track job as head of acquisitions at the College of Charleston. My small staff included three LTA IIIs. Barely a year later, in 1980, I decided to expand the Charleston Conference, since I was receiving a lot of questions and encouragement to do so.

Since I was hired in a tenure-track position, I wanted to see if this was an avenue to help me for tenure. I have to admit that a lot of what I do is based on my instinct. After all, my instinct has never failed me in seventy-five years (except for my first marriage).

The 1981 Conference

The conference seemed to have hit a nerve of need. There was a lot of interest in rare books, but also in acquiring more types of books for more types of libraries.

In 1981, I decided to try expanding the meeting. This time, I asked those who had come to the first meeting to invite friends to this second meeting about acquiring all types of books (not just rare books) for libraries. I also invited local colleagues. The new dean of continuing education had new office space and gave me a larger classroom for the 1981 conference. I charged as little as possible in order to pay the fees of the Center for Continuing Education and make the conference affordable for attendees.

We had twice as many attendees in 1981 as we did in 1980.

Shirley Davidson, my awesome LTA, helped assemble packets and refreshments. Shirley and Regina Semko and I located people for hire or volunteers for a free conference registration to help with registration and preparing registration packets. As the number of attendees grew, Shirley and Regina and I would locate more volunteers. The conference would continue to be run at the Center for Continuing Education until 1989 when we moved to the Lightsey Center.

Much of the excitement of the 1981 conference was heightened by discussion of the unanimous Supreme Court decision in *Thor Power Tool Company v. Commissioner* which had been decided in January 1979. The Court upheld IRS regulations limiting how taxpayers could write down inventory. This caused US publishers and booksellers to be much quicker to destroy stocks of poorly selling books in order to realize a taxable loss. In the past, poorly selling books would have been kept in stock but written down to reflect the fact that not all of them were expected to sell. To write down is an accounting treatment that recognizes the reduced value of an impaired asset; that is, an asset that can't be sold at the same price. This gave us all a glimpse of the developing marketplace we were entering.

I Was a New Mother

In 1982, my daughter Ileana was born. She was a delight; my son Raymond was ecstatic. He had been praying for a sibling for several years! My husband Bruce and I and our son Raymond adored the new baby. She was breastfeeding nicely and loved to put all the toys in her mouth! I was enjoying my short leave of absence with few interruptions. We were all hunky-dory. I was adjusting to it all, getting my bearings in what would hopefully become a long and productive career.

Professional Squabbles

At the library, we were settling in under the new director, but we still squabbled about small things.

Was a director *primus inter pares* or an absolute boss? Was library work a cooperative endeavor like an academic department, or a top-down management of a business? Should librarians be treated as faculty and thus engage in research and professional development? Should individual libraries innovate or slavishly copy the Tier 1 libraries for safety at accreditation time?

As we debated these questions, I was finding my way into a philosophy that would guide my work over many years to come: I have always managed by letting people work to their strengths and not according to a rigid template. I have always been enough on top of my employees' work that I knew how they were doing without resorting to a time clock.

As to individual versus herd behavior, I have always advocated letting a thousand flowers bloom.

During this period, there was a lot of turmoil among the college administrators and faculty, and a lot of internal change. The president resigned, an interim president was appointed, and a vice president was appointed from a library in our South Carolina community. There was a lot of stress and infighting. In the 1980s and 1990s, the faculty senate structure of representation from academic departments at large was in place. Before 1993, faculty governance was through full faculty meetings of all College of Charleston faculty. In 1993, a faculty senate was created and became the primary legislative body. I was a senator, and I remember the jockeying during this time. I wasn't into all the politics. After Ileana was born, I had other priorities.

Chapter 4

GROWING THE CONFERENCE (1983–1989)

The 1983 conference was at the top of my list. It was the first with a theme. "Collection Development in the '80s" was held May 12–13 in the Center for Continuing Education at the College of Charleston. The registration fee was $50 for the two-day conference or $25 for one day. That was the year of the first cocktail party sponsored by EBSCO's Nancy Rogers in her hotel room.

In those early years, when I was still young and lively, I would gather a big crowd to go to the No Name Café at night to drink and dance. Waitresses dressed as cheerleaders would climb up on the bar and dance high kicks like Rockettes. Those librarians and vendors will let loose, and gossip detailed many a *sub rosa* romance. For those reading, you know who you are.

In 1985 (theme: "More Than You Ever Wanted to Know about Finances") Steve Johnson (Clemson) presented his first beer-tasting workshop at the Francis Marion Hotel. Brian Cox (Elsevier) was one of the attendees among many.

In 1986, the college hired an excellent new president, Harry Lightsey, followed the next year by a new provost,

Conrad Festa, who was very hands-on. All the tension dissipated.

Conrad Festa invited many of us to lunch in separate groups. He seemed to have noticed the Charleston Conference. Many years later, he would even offer me the opportunity to have a second conference for teaching faculty in southern colleges.

With the theme "External Influences on Acquisitions and Collection Development," 1986 was our first year with more than one hundred attendees, and the first time Lyman Newlin was a speaker.

Lyman was one of the most energetic, charming, wonderful old men I have ever known. Lyman never ran out of energy or stories. Or beer. He rode the train wherever he went. I'm not sure he could drive. You couldn't start a conversation with him without his mentioning his favorite jobs. His dream job in his youth was at Kroch's and Brentano's, the largest bookstore in Chicago. To him, it was a magic Ali Baba's cavern of knowledge.

Later, Lyman would write a column for *Against the Grain*, "Papa Lyman Remembers." They were always charming and had details of Chicago and the Great Depression. But he never learned to type and would handwrite them on a legal pad, with inserts and arrows and near gibberish that I had to transcribe. Maddening. In his last years, Lyman used a wheelchair, but still rode the train down and motored around the hotel in a mobility scooter.

But back to 1987: we welcomed our first international participants, from the UK and Africa, as well as participants from thirty-six states. It was Lyman Newlin who introduced me to the legend Richard Abel, an earnest innovator who saw the potential of research libraries purchasing the same group of academic books and was in attendance that year. He brought with him his "approval plan," in which academic libraries could receive notices of the books or, even better, the actual printed books, to select for their library collections. A major focus: they could peruse the books and return what they did not want to keep or pay for.

It was a heady time. Lyman and Richard Abel and their colleagues felt they had done an early Google-type thing with the approval plan and totally roiled the bookselling market for libraries. They were masters of the library book universe with a big expense account from investors.

Another serious topic at the 1987 conference was European pricing versus American pricing of books, which was under discussion by Deana Astle and Chuck Hamaker.[1] This was to continue to be discussed and debated for many future years.

In 1988, we had the first Hyde Park Corner session, which allowed attendees to write up a statement for what they wanted to discuss. It was decided by a small group what topics to cover. The session was later turned into a formal Oxford debate. The idea was conceived by Rick Anderson, who is the emcee for all the conference debates.

Hyde Park in London is popular for excursions and demonstrations. Later, Speakers' Corner, a place for free expression, was established. This was our "lucky seventh" annual conference.

But it was the following year that would really test our luck.

Hurricane Hugo: 1989

In 1985, we shifted the conference date from May to November purely because there was a slot unoccupied by other conferences.

Big conferences like the American Library Association (ALA) tended to seek the cheapest hotel rates. That meant Chicago in a January blizzard and San Antonio in prostrating heat. Attendees were essentially stranded in their hotels clinging to heat or cool.

Charleston has some pretty vile weather as well. Summers are oppressive humidity and burning sun. Winters have cold winds blowing off the harbor. But November…

November is one of those in-between months where the weather is typically glorious. Folks wander around in shirtsleeves under a robin's egg blue sky. This is the weather where the lucky visitor vows to move here, thinking it's heaven.

In all the years, we've only had one freezing temperature conference. And, of course, there's hurricane season.

Folks who relocate here soon discover what a tense time that is, watching the storm tracks and seeing lower South Carolina sticking out on the map just inviting devastation.

Around that time, I had begun to think that conference folks needed a way to keep in touch more than once a year. I envisioned a stenographed four-page broadsheet-like newsletter with news from the conference attendees. I was friends with Steve Johnson, acquisitions librarian at Clemson, who had a subscription beer newsletter, so he offered to help.

I started a bank account and devoted one hundred of my own dollars to it, and in March 1989, *Against the Grain* was born, ten pages, five ounces.

Steve and I were working on *Against the Grain* five months later, on September 25, 1989, when Hurricane Hugo, a Category 5 Atlantic hurricane, hit Awendaw Island. Awendaw is just twenty miles from Sullivan's Island. Sullivan's Island is twenty minutes from Charleston. I was living in Charleston on the Citadel campus back then.

People who know about hurricanes know how unpredictable they are, so Steve and I were pretty nonchalant. We continued to work on *Against the Grain* even though the hurricane was predicted to hit Charleston. Eventually, though, Bruce and our two children and the dog, along with my iMac and many, many floppy disks and paperwork, set out of Charleston. The cadets had been evacuated from the Citadel campus, neighbors had gone elsewhere, the neighborhoods were spookily quiet, birds weren't singing, and people were securing their boats, tables, chairs, and anything that could blow away.

We stayed in Leesville, SC, two hours west of Charleston, a delightful, friendly place, and watched the rain and wind pound down. We watched and listened to the weather reports which told us to stay away from Charleston. It took us three days before we decided to head back to Charleston.

Everything had changed. Street signs and streetlights were out, and power lines and fallen trees and limbs were everywhere. Our house at the Citadel had survived miraculously, and even our palmetto tree was still standing. Some others weren't so lucky. I do remember my son Raymond was fourteen and devastated that we evacuated because several of his friends stayed. Those friends were a source for us to learn how the campus and Charleston were doing. The president of the Citadel, General Watts, who had just come to Charleston four months before, arranged to keep the campus active. The cadets had all been sent home, so there was a lot of food to keep from spoiling. My children remember the time fondly, with tons of food in the cafeteria! No lights or electricity, so we used candles.

It was late September, and I was getting lots of phone calls asking about the status of the conference, which was only six weeks away. We had scheduled the Mills House Hotel in downtown Charleston for the conference. It was impossible to drive or take transportation, so I walked downtown to the Mills. It was hard to recognize where you were. It was like Charleston civilization had been destroyed!

Still, thankfully, everyone at the Mills Hotel was upbeat and assured me that the conference could go on! It was a rough six weeks as the city tried to return to normal, fixing traffic lights and signage, getting electric power back after six weeks of darkness. Returning to our offices, there was determination in the air; all was upbeat and positive.

And the conference did indeed go on in the Mills House Hotel in downtown Charleston. We apologized that the conference was "too big" with more than three hundred attendees.

The theme was "Remembrance of Things Past." Given all that we'd lost during Hurricane Hugo, this was an appropriate and prescient theme! The keynote speaker was the awesome Edwin Shelock of the Royal Society of Chemistry. Other speakers included: Meta Nissley (Cal State, Chico), Rick van Orden (OCLC), Marcia Tuttle (UNC-CH), Pieter Bolman (Pergamon Press), Michael Keller (Yale), Bob Mastejulia (Baker & Taylor), Barbara Meyers (Meyers Consulting), Sandra Paul (SKP Associates), Duane Webster (Association of Research Libraries), Jolanda von Hagen (Springer Verlag NY), Mary McLaren (University of Kentucky), and Barbara Winters (Virginia Commonwealth University).

Topics on the program included: publish or perish, intellectual property rights, antitrust issues, the emergence of European journal publishing, the ARL project on serial pricing, automated acquisitions systems.[2]

Also there were sessions on electronic ordering and book and journal pricing.

(All of the conference programs that we could locate are loaded online at the Charleston Hub: www.charleston-hub.com.)

That year, we had the first and only Spirit of Charleston Dinner boat cruise and did a lot of dancing! We also had a Saturday morning session at the Dock Street Theater, and a beer and wine reception at the Blacklock House on Bull Street.

Katina's Big Booboo!

This was also the time of Katina's big booboo!

In those first years (1980–89) we moved venues for the conference frequently depending on availability and room sizes needed.

In 1990, we had been moved to the Lightsey Conference Center, which had been a Sears store previously, so there was a lot of movement and renovation going on. Unfortunately, the renovators had not allowed for enough restrooms, and we had a houseful! There were lots of complaints, especially from the women. In desperation, I announced the decision that the men's room would be opened to women, and that men could use the restroom in the college restaurant across the way! Gosh! Pretty nervy!

But people were good-spirited enough to obey my decision. And thank goodness that we never had to use that facility again, since the conference got larger, and we had to change venues!

Chapter 5

THE LIBRARY WORLD IN THE 1970S AND 1980S

Let's turn our attention for a moment from the Charleston Conference history to the library world more broadly. Back in the 1970s, the library world as we know it was not at all mature. I remember the elderly head of cataloging at a nearby library being vehemently against joining an unknown upstart unincorporated organization called the Online Computer Library Center (OCLC). Back then, acquisitions was a fledgling field for a medium-sized academic library.

In retrospect, I was entering a developing library and technology world. Imagine.

New Technologies

This was the era of the Sony Walkman, floppy disks, Pong (arcade game), the Apple II, the first digital camera and first cellphone call, audio and video cassette recorders, email, the first microprocessors, videogames, cordless phones, personal computers, and microwave ovens.

Computers were in their infancy. MITS Altair 8800 kit, BASIC programming language, the digital camera, Microsoft, and the Apple computer had all come on the scene. But most of us were still using manual typewriters. At the college library, there was only one electric typewriter in the entire building.

How Were Books Ordered Back Then?

In those days, libraries would order from wholesalers like Baker & Taylor and Ingram. Most libraries didn't purchase directly from authors, or even publishers. Wholesalers would offer you a sizable discount if you bought books from them, and the more books, the bigger the discount. It was competitive. I remember being called or visited or wined and dined by many sales representatives from the big wholesalers, primarily since we were buying more academic books. Baker & Taylor and Ingram supplied books largely for public libraries.

Thankfully, a wonderful sales rep from Midwest Library Services called on me. I learned that the college had done some ordering from Midwest from my fabulous LTA Shirley Davidson. We began to get packets of xeroxed cards with information on new books that were available for purchase. It was before the approval plan, so we would sometimes call or send in a snail mail order for a specific book.

Publisher Commercialization Policies and Issues

The commercial publishers' print subscription model was very simple but frustrating to the library community. The pricing model meant that the subscription price of the journal was established by each publisher.

The Women's Movement

By the late 1970s, librarianship was coming into its own as a profession.

Starting in the 1960s, the growth of the women's movement had put pressure on colleges to have female faculty. Nationwide, colleges granted faculty status to the professional librarians, which gave them a quick headcount of women.

But the women's movement produced female PhDs in all the subject areas, and the urgency was no longer there. Administrators longed to have people they could boss around, since the academic faculty are always fairly untouchable. And those librarians only held the master of library and information science (MLS) degree.

Thus, a retrograde movement began. I have heard one of the most prominent library directors in the nation proclaim he'd get rid of tenure for librarians if he could. Meaning, buck him and you're gone the next year.

Book Acquisition

As I had been planning the first Charleston Conference, I started trying to learn how to recognize a rare book. At the same time, I was trying to learn how to buy any book whatsoever for the library! LTA Shirley knew a lot, but we both knew there was a lot to learn. I soon learned that book acquisition was different from medical librarianship! Back then, book ordering by libraries was just getting started. There were very few established library tools.

So where to begin when you know nothing about acquiring books? How did you know what to order, and if you had it in the collection already, and from whom should you order? Were your earlier acquisitions reflected in the card catalog? I had zero experience, so I started digging around. There were a few resources out there! Here are some resources that were being developed and were available back then.

The First Card Catalog

I learned that in 1840 Harvard's Ezra Abbot created the first modern card catalog. His associate, Charles Cutter, who became the librarian at the Boston Athenaeum in 1868, created a new scheme that was later the basis for the Library of Congress cataloging system. Cutter was overshadowed by Melvil Dewey, whose controlled vocabulary consisted of numerical values.[1]

The CBI and Library of Congress National Union Catalog

In 1898, Halsey William Wilson was a student working his way through the University of Minnesota. With a colleague, he started a bookselling business for educators and students at the university. Tired of searching through individual publishers' catalogs, he conceived of the Cumulative Book Index (CBI), a comprehensive alphabetical list of books currently published in English by author, title, and subject, which was published in 1898–99. We did have a copy of the CBI in the library, and I used it frequently to locate cataloging and subject information about books. An anecdote: I remember that one of the major volumes of the 754-volume set was missing and could not be purchased separately. That was when we relied on interlibrary loan, because we couldn't find our copy anywhere.

Publishers Weekly

The library had recently taken out a subscription to *Publishers Weekly* (*PW*), which had been established in 1872 by bibliographer Frederick Leypoldt and was intended for booksellers. It was a compilation of information about newly published books collected from publishers and other sources. He sold *Publishers Weekly* in 1878–79 to his friend Richard Rogers Bowker. *PW* is an essential resource to keep up with all publishing gossip and information.

The Bookman

In 1895, *The Bookman* appeared in New York. Frank H. Dodd (Dodd, Mead and Company) had established it with Harry Peck as the first editor (1895–1906). Peck created America's first bestseller list. *The Bookman* list ran from 1895 to 1918 and is the only comprehensive source of annual bestsellers of the US from 1895 to 1912, when *PW* began publishing its own bestseller list. I consulted the bestseller lists frequently to learn which books to order for the library.

MARC and Henriette Avram

In the 1970s, libraries began to embrace MARC (machine-readable cataloging) and the computer catalog. The College of Charleston Library followed suit in order to keep up with what was going on in library catalogs. Between 1965 and 1968, American computer scientist and visionary Henriette Avram developed MARC, making it possible to create records that could be read by computers and shared.

We also had been ordering using Midwest slip notices of newly published books.

Online Computer Library Center

In 1967, OCLC was founded as a nonprofit membership organization by Fred Kilgour who was an American, former Yale University Medical School Librarian, and educator. Kilgour came to be known as the founding director of OCLC, an international computer library network and database. Initially, it was limited to institutions in Ohio, but in 1978 a new governance structure allowed other states to join. In 2002 the governance structure would be modified again to accommodate participation from outside the US. I was unable to locate when the College of Charleston joined OCLC. Perhaps 2002 or 2003?

Books In Print

Books In Print, the most important book-buying tool, was published in 1977. Coincidentally, the Spoleto Festival USA opened in the Charleston Civic Auditorium, later the Gaillard Center, that same year, and the first computer programming languages were announced. The Spoleto Festival USA was founded in 1977 by Pulitzer

Prize-winning composer Gian Carlo Menotti. He wanted to establish a counterpart to the Festival dei Due Mondi in Spoleto, Italy. Since Bruce and I are opera lovers, we immediately got tickets and a babysitter for the very first opera here in Charleston, Verdi's *La traviata*. What a thrill!

Librarian of Congress

But most important of all, in 1870 Ainsworth Rand Spofford was Librarian of Congress. The Copyright Act of 1870 requires that materials registered for copyright be deposited with the Library, so the catalog began growing fast! With the opening of a new library building, Herbert Putnam became Librarian in 1899, and a new cataloging division was created. In 1901 Putnam sent a memo to more than four hundred libraries announcing the sale of its printed catalog cards. This service was wildly popular and made the Library the standard-bearer, since libraries across the country could possess the same quality cataloging. I do remember when Robert Maxwell was trying to buy Putnam, the publishing company. He offered something like $35,000 for it. Putnam attended the Charleston Conference back at the beginning.

In 1975 historian Daniel J. Boorstin was appointed Librarian of Congress. His objective was greater public visibility for the institution. He founded the Center for the Book in 1977 to promote books, reading, and libraries and the study of books. There are now affiliate centers in all fifty states. The South Carolina Center for the Book started getting affiliate centers in 1984.

Conclusion

The '80s saw the invention of personal computers, microchips, the first laptop computers, the first listserv, cellphones, CDs, Microsoft Windows, and the Apple Macintosh.

The Charleston Conference wasn't far behind. We had a few computer workstations for attendees. Arranging for enough connections for as many as over one hundred attendees was challenging! There were also several library listservs.

The conference seemed to be getting a regular place on the academic calendar. We had some spectacular papers get newsworthy attention. Stephen Rhind-Tutt (around 1987) gave a paper outlining pricing models and strategies that was cited for many years; Jerry Cowhig of the Institute of Physics gave a riveting physics explanation of how the cookie crumbles in certain ways, which was even covered by the London *Financial Times*; and Janet Flowers's summary of the 2004 conference reflects admirably on the program and speakers.

I have to give a shoutout to *Library Journal*, the Association of College and Research Libraries, *Against the Grain*, *Serials Review*, and many publications that kept the conference on their reporting radar.

Part 2

1989–2005: The Middle

Chapter 6

TECHNOLOGY TAKES CHARGE

Many technological changes happened in the 1990s. The old world ended, and the new one began!

The first web browser, "www," the internet, text messaging, growing power, the first PlayStation; Amazon opened its online bookshop in 1995; the Napster music streaming service, and rise of bloggers; cable channels were competing for ratings 24/7.

My Life Among Books

I haven't mentioned that my husband Bruce and I were fiction writers in our spare and dreamy time.

When we moved to Charleston, it was the most romantic, rundown city with authors and all sorts of people and characters everywhere.

It was barely a fourth of its current size. Every building had a fascinating history. The Charleston Library Society was a subscription library founded in 1748, the third in America. Its current location is in a Beaux Arts building on lower King Street, just above the Broad Street home of Dr. John Lining, who studied botany, meteorology, and human metabolism. He kept detailed records of his health and hoped to establish a connection between the effects of weather conditions on bodily functions and disease. He conducted the first weather records for 1738–53.

The South Carolina Historical Society was in the historic Fireproof Building on Meeting Street, holding artifacts and documents from three hundred and fifty years of history. The collection has recently been moved to the College of Charleston, but in the '80s it was an adventure to discover some of the documents and history from the past.

In 1980, there were only about five restaurants in the town, and you could easily get a parking space in the Market on Saturday night. On Friday night, all the Charleston gentry class could be found dining at Henry's on the Market, the oldest restaurant in the state, although it only dated to 1932. It was famous for crab-stuffed flounder surrounded by a wall of mashed potatoes.

Henry's bar was a wonderful place of eclectic nautical junk. Robert Marks held court there every afternoon over Bloody Marys, until he would stagger home to Tradd Street. Marks was a polymath who wrote books on everything from music to mathematics. Late in life, he began to write pornography as John Colleton, his most famous being *The Trembling of a Leaf.* Smut censorship had vanished in the '70s, and he was published by Pocket, sold in airports, and made quite a bit of money.

As authors, Bruce and I were intrigued and wanted to meet him. Since I was in charge of locating gift books for the college library, I introduced myself to him and said we were interested in his book collections. He invited me to his Tradd Street house more than once. What a place and book collection! Later, after his death, our Special Collections department was gifted many of his books. Moving right along, I figured as Milton Berle said: "If opportunity doesn't knock, build a door." Since my husband had written a short story, I crossed my fingers and sent it to Robert Marks for comments. He liked it enough to pass it to Harriet McDougal, a Charlestonian who was acquiring books for New York publishers.

Harriet later married Jim Rigney and made him into superstar author Robert Jordan with the *Wheel of Time* series. But that was in the future. Right then, she had just moved from NYC to an inherited ancient home on Tradd Street with a ghost in the carriage house, and was fighting with a broken water heater.

We sat at the dining room table, and she offered me a contract to write a book. That was the kind of serendipity that we somehow expected of the magic city.

I have to put on my honest face here: my husband was the writer, and my only claim was as editor. Still, he insisted that I take the responsibility as the author. Bruce is a much better showman than I, and I regret that he didn't come forward. Admittedly, we were young and unknown.

Harriet brokered the first manuscript—*Youngblood* (1982)—with few changes to Tom Doherty at Tor.

I remember seeing it in an airport bookstore for the first time. That will give you a thrill. Airport reads. Fantasy took flight. "I wanna be a paperback writer."

We acquired Janet Manus as a literary agent, and the magic continued through the '80s and into the '90s. Janet's husband was an entertainment lawyer, and we dined with them at the Friar's Club. He had just acquired Kool and the Gang as clients.

I visited Janet's Connecticut country home where the plutocrat inventor of the Veg-O-Matic was also a guest and a hilarious raconteur.

We published under the pen names Athena Alexis and Katina Alexis, the 'A' name selected because novels were lined up alphabetically in the then thriving bookstore chains like B. Dalton and Doubleday.

Our very first book (*Along Came a Spider*) was published by Dell and had been translated into several languages. Unfortunately, we and the publisher had chosen the same title that James Patterson had for one of his new books, so the publisher got cold feet. That shouldn't have caused us to give up hope, but instead we switched genres, which wasn't a profitable idea. We still had our jobs and kept writing. Next was *Souls* (Pocket) in 1992, followed by many others. *Scorpion* (Dorchester Leisure Books) followed in 1996. *Witch* (Pocket) was published in 1990 in multiple foreign languages. Seeing your title in German (*Hexe*) and Icelandic will give one a frisson.

Backing Up

By 1986, despite my work at the library and moonlighting as an author, I was getting restless. I had even applied to start my doctorate in library science at UNC-Chapel Hill. At the same time, there was an entrepreneur who wanted me to start another conference for libraries like the Charleston Conference, but to make it private and not allied with the College of Charleston, probably more focused on authors across the US. He thought there was interest in a unique librarians' conference. I think he also thought the meeting should move out of Charleston and have a more central location. He was a businessman and very charming, but he was focused on starting his new business, and I certainly didn't blame his decisions.

Since I had a new child who was nine months old, I quickly realized library school was unrealistic. Instead, I agreed to be a consultant to let the entrepreneur plan to start Acquisitions 1990 in St. Louis. If they used my name, I wanted some power.

Of course, I had no idea how to do this. I was just young and excited and maybe a little bored; St. Louis seemed like a delightful place with the famous Gateway Arch. It was also the location of Anthony Garnett's famous collection of rare books, which I had visited before. Anthony was a flamboyant Englishman who was a very literary rare bookseller. He had visited our library frequently with specific rare books or prospective lists of rare books to sell. I wasn't able and knew that I didn't have the expertise to make rare book decisions, so these decisions were left to the library director.

I gathered the entrepreneur knew Anthony and wanted to control the arrangement; he seemed to want me for my name, such as it was, and contacts, which seemed OK to me. There was no contract to sign. I suppose this would make a great textbook case study of what not to do in business.

Speaking of connections, I had a growing group of contacts for both the St. Louis conference and the Charleston Conference. I was meeting many people for the first time. I remember meeting the learned, energetic Sara Miller McCune and her feisty mother outside the Mills House Hotel with the delightfully crusty Lyman Newlin, who was working for Coutts. He knew everybody!

I located a keynote for the Acquisitions 1990 St. Louis conference and arranged to share invitations with my contact lists. Things seemed to be moving along, until unknown family problems for the entrepreneur derailed the planning for the St. Louis conference.

Instead, I decided to plan for the upcoming Charleston Conferences.

I had worked with many women who had helped me with the Charleston Conference in the 1980s: Regina Semko, Judy Webster, Dorinda Harmon. And countless kudos to them and all kudos to the organizers of the 1990 conference: Dorinda Harmon, Allison Cleveland, Joni Rouse, Barbara Dean, Heather Miller, and Judy Webster, and many others! There are some vignettes about them all.

According to the FAQ (the first for the Charleston Conference), there were four hundred and thirty people (publishers, vendors, and librarians) registered to attend the 1990 Charleston Conference: "Issues in Book and Serial Acquisition: The Pure and Simple Truth," November 8–10. We were meeting in the Lightsey Conference Center of the College of Charleston. The Francis Marion Hotel had arranged to construct an entrance to the hotel from the Conference Center.

The 1990 Charleston Conference was the TENTH. We had another Hyde Park Corner discussion, and the innovatively creative Marcia Tuttle began the *Newsletter on Serials Pricing Issues (NOSPI)* which led to much discussion. We had preconferences for the first time! And a rump session after the conference was over.

Why a rump session? I was beginning to sense that we were losing the "togetherness" that we had when the conference was only two days and attended by fewer people. I hoped that the rump session could remind people of the intimacy that we had felt when the conference first started. Many of my colleagues were leery of the idea of the rump session, but we kept it up until it disappeared during the pandemic.

I suppose I should have also been leery of agreeing to have a second conference to possibly compete with the Charleston Conference, but as Sophia Loren says, "Mistakes are part of the dues one pays for old age."

The theme of the 1990 Charleston Conference was from Oscar Wilde: "The Pure and Simple Truth is rarely pure and never simple." Technology was seriously impacting our otherwise seemingly stable pure and simple world.

Gordon Graham, once CEO of Butterworths, now the editor of *LOGOS*, a new magazine, gave the keynote address with Carol Chamberlain from Penn State University: "Gatekeepers and Information: Publisher and Librarian: The Same Only Different."

Registration was brisk, and the proceedings were published in *Library Acquisitions: Practice & Theory*.[1]

In retrospect I decided to focus on the Charleston Conference rather than the St. Louis conferences. The Charleston Conference was growing physically and operationally. We had established the month of November on the annual conference calendar, and we were supported by the same continuing staff members.

In the library, my awesome serials librarian colleague had resigned for another job. I was asked to take over the administration of the serials department temporarily. I was to learn that the serials department was quite different from the acquisitions department operationally. In acquisitions we ordered books and paid invoices for books that we had ordered, and our primary functions were: a) to verify what we wanted to order; b) to order it from a vendor; c) to follow up on all open orders; d) to receive items; e) verify that the item we received was the correct item; and f) to pay for it.

Not the case with serials. Serial orders are continuing, basically standing orders. Many are ordered from different jobbers or publishers. Prices can be fluid and discounts are negotiated. Prices and jobbers change frequently.

In the serials department, we had continuing orders for many serials that we received at different times during the year. I soon learned that we had stacks of unpaid invoices from serials vendors. This was unacceptable! Our faculty relied on our keeping up our orders for subscriptions! All the outstanding bills had to be paid promptly!

Back to Reality!

The next Charleston Conference was slated to be held in 1991 with the theme "And I Am Right and You Are Right, Too-Loo-Ra-Lay" from Gilbert and Sullivan's operetta *The Mikado*, which captured the ways in which publishers, vendors, and librarians differ. We hosted the first preconference and the first Lively Lunch. We had established a small group of "conference directors" who had worked together on earlier conferences and could express opinions freely without rancor or conflict.

I am not sure of the very first Charleston Conference that Anthony Watkinson emceed! But it must have been in the late 1980s. Anthony very quickly became the emcee of the conference for years! Anthony is a great emcee, always ready with a quip, a question, an introduction, or a statement. He knows everybody and knows exactly how to charm his audience!

The 1992 conference theme was "The Medium Is the Message." We had our first waiting list for participants, which we'd capped at 383.

Things were going well, until my office telephone rang and I answered it! An official-sounding woman whom I did not know said she was from the American Library Association. She said I had been nominated to run for ALA president in 1992. I nearly dropped the phone. For background, I had been a member of ALA for several years, but I had never had an official appointment of any type. This should have been a clue to say no, no, no. But as Napoleon once said: "In politics, stupidity is not a handicap." My husband said he would divorce me if I didn't run (NOT!) and there were others who thought I should run. Still, I said no.

But the woman called back several weeks later to ask me again! Another clue to say no! Maybe I was losing my mind? In fact, I am sure that I did lose my mind, because in 1992 I agreed to run for ALA president. They did not and would not tell me who I was running against, which should have been the final clue, but I was young and naive, so I said yes, stupidly. Turns out I was running against the future Librarian of Congress, Carla Hayden!

I do remember sharing my hotel room with two colleagues and sleeping on the pullout sofa in our hotel room. Longtime friend Sandy Paul was my campaign manager— kudos to her! Sandy and I had to meet with all the committees and subcommittees and whatevers of ALA. Usually the meetings were informal with no refreshments or introductions. It was a grueling process. Sandy and I met all during the ALA week, with the chairs of countless committees wanting to know if I supported their positions on specific issues like ALA governance, funding for increased library services, drug use, lack of and need for childcare, pay equity, sexual harassment, and so on.

There was a big onstage debate with a lot of my supporters cheering me on. I have to say that I was happy to make it through! Many good friends—Sandy Paul, Becky Lenzini, Ward Shaw, Mitch Friedman, Helen Henderson, Chris Lemy, and many, many others—encouraged me on!

In the end, I got a good number of votes, but thank heavens that I lost! Whew! The end of my short-lived political career.

While it was a relief not to win the election, it would have been an interesting perch from which to observe the rapid and transformative changes that would unfold over the next decade.

It was probably six years later that *The Charleston Advisor* was founded. In 1999, I had taken over the serials section of the library as well as acquisitions. I was trying to suggest what we should consider for purchase. That led me to contemplate the need for a reviewing publication of available electronic serial products, of which there were many. I started discussing this with a charming friend, Becky Lenzini, who was working at the Faxon Company, a serials supplier to libraries and a competitor, briefly, to EBSCO. Becky had run a great product selection workshop at UNC-Chapel Hill that I attended.

Everybody loves Becky. She is very attractive, vivacious, smiling, and positive. She always becomes informed and knows what's going on. After much back-and-forth, we came up with *The Charleston Advisor*, a critical review resource of electronic products for information professionals. This launched in July 1999 as a peer-reviewed publication published by the Charleston Company (Becky Lenzini and Ward Shaw), and Bruce and Katina Strauch with the Charleston Information Group, edited by George Machovec (executive director of the Colorado Alliance of Research Libraries). The successful publication was acquired from Becky, Ward, Katina, and Bruce in 2022 by the publisher Annual Reviews. There was always some confusion around the Charleston Company (Becky and Ward) and the Charleston Information Group (Katina and Bruce), and that's my fault!

Around this time, I continued to get interesting calls from companies that had been watching the conference and *Against the Grain* (*ATG*). Several seemed interested in buying us. We were new and unique.

Even in the early '80s, Duncan Spence, a rich guy with vineyards in South Africa (and a UNC-Charlotte girlfriend), John Cox, and Charles Germain took me to lunch at a brand-new restaurant on Queen Street across from the Mills House Hotel in downtown Charleston, Poogan's Porch, which still exists. They told me I could take the advertising money from *ATG* at that time, approximately $50,000. Then I was supposed to start three new journals, which they would own. Yeah, sure.

Next came two gentlemen from *Library Journal*. They floated many offer amounts but never put anything in writing. They were persistent! Finally, one of them called me to make an offer, but I turned him down. Seemed very unprofessional, and I guess they thought I didn't know what I was doing. No doubt about it.

Now ALA was sniffing around. One guy in charge told me to tell him what I wanted, and they would try to get it. But they never put a formal offer out there either. Whatever.

Besides, it wasn't the right time to sell. I didn't want the conference to become part of a venture capital company or acquisition. I feared profit would be favored over partnership or content. It was clear to me that the conference would be changed, sliced and diced, expanded, and resold rather than developed for loyal companies in the scholarly communication chain.

But I continued to hear from various entrepreneurs about completing various projects, and some offers were more appealing than others.

About that time, one of my boss's assistants offered me the job as director of the college's Marine Resources Library (MRL) out on Fort Johnson. It was a small library in an idyllic setting on the water with a lot of research faculty whom I knew working there. I was tempted but unsure of the long-term stability of the place, since it was very grant-dependent. The current sitting MRL Librarian, Helen Ivy, a longtime colleague, had done much work to make it very viable. I did not want to upset the apple cart.

In 1999, Mario Casalini flew Bruce and me to Fiesole, Italy to consider starting a conference in Europe. He had attended many Charleston Conferences. He was the most urbane, elegant, cultured, courteous gentleman I have ever known. He always brought me roses. He had a daughter, Barbara, and a son, Michele. He was known all over the world and even in the United States. As the Charleston Conference became more of a must-attend conference, he started coming regularly.

One afternoon, he invited Bruce and me to come to his home in Fiesole, Italy. He was interested in the possibility of starting a Charleston-like conference in Italy. Italy is an awesome place and soon replaced Paris and Greece in our preferences. I remember landing in Fiesole late one night. The plane was late, so we hadn't had time to get Italian money! But the Italians were wonderful and took us to the awesomely elegant Pensione Bencista across the way from the Casalini estate. The Casalinis were very cultured and European. They spoke Italian and German and were proficient in many more languages. Michael Keller was a great mutual friend, and we all shared many good times together.

Sadly, Mario died before the first retreat, but at Michael's suggestion, we planted an olive tree on the Casalini property, which lives on. My husband also painted a fabulous portrait of Mario, which we gave to his wife. We have a copy hanging in our Sullivan's Island home. It can be seen in the photo section on page 80.

The first Fiesole Retreat was in 1999. We have had a Fiesole Retreat every year for the past twenty-four years, all in different parts of the world. Every fourth year, the retreat returns to Fiesole. Here are other cities where there have been Fiesole Retreats: Oxford, Amsterdam, Lund, Melbourne, Hong Kong, Leuven, Glasgow, St. Petersburg, Cambridge, Singapore, Berlin, Barcelona, Lille, Basel, Athens, Cape Town.

Michele Casalini has taken over management of the retreat and is doing a great job. The last retreat was in South Africa, and another one is being planned. The next one (2025) will be held in Fiesole and will celebrate the twenty-fifth anniversary of the event![2] Leah Hinds, representing the Charleston Hub, is working with them on the planning committee.

This period of my career coincided with what would be dubbed "The Formative Years of Digital Libraries," by William Y. Arms (Cornell Computer Science Department), referring to the transformative shift of libraries from housing collections of books and journals to housing digital collections.[3]

Many years ago, I remember completing several library school programming assignments which involved punch cards! During the 1980s, Xerox copiers had led to word processors, and in 1992, the conference theme, "The Medium Is the Message," was a response to changes in document formats and delivery. The following year, with the theme "Bubble, Bubble Toil and Trouble," (inspired by

Heather Miller) we wrestled with the question whether these changes were good or bad.

The digital era had brought platforms that allowed us to order and read much of what we wanted. We were moving from the traditional card catalog to web-based searching and resources. Barcode-scanning was replacing stamping due dates on circulating books. Instead of waiting weeks for an interlibrary loan, borrowing was being expedited quickly. We had access to online course content.

In the 1994 theme, "The Savage Marketplace," competition and adversity reared their heads.

Still Crazy After All These Words

In 1995, we were indeed "Still Crazy After All These Words," that year's conference theme. All that was happening in the scholarly communications space made me ready to hire two of my colleagues to help us temporarily. In the serials section of the library, which I had just been hired to take over, we were rewriting and filling several LTA positions.

There were hundreds of unpaid invoices to be verified and prepared for payment. Our team got through it all—whew!

In 1996 ("Money Talks"—You'd better believe it!) I had a small staff and budget for my library job, but I needed money beyond my own for the Charleston Conference. Several booksellers and serial vendors came forward to offer to help with mailings and expenses. I also had plenty of volunteers to recruit speakers and even more volunteers.

By 1997, "Learning From Our Mistakes," we (I should say I) had made our/my share of mistakes. For one, I had told a speaker they could speak at a certain time, and the time slot was already occupied by someone else! When the time came to publicize the program, it was obvious. OOPS! My face was highly and very red!

1998's theme, "We Want More For Less," reflected the fact that we librarians had realized the value of our assets. We had content that was necessary for businesses and other companies to continue to provide. They had to work with us.

1999: "And the Beat Goes On." The Charleston Conference that year included several presentations about the role of e-books and their usage. *The Charleston Report* outlined general opinion on e-books from the Charleston 1999 conference: "General opinion is that they are coming faster than we think, but standards are needed and more experience is required. Some public libraries are investing in e-book collections available for checkout to patrons; others are buying e-books just for staff use in order to get up to speed."[4]

Also, Charles Watkinson had worked with David Brown's book distribution warehouse in the US to deal with the emerging world of e-books and distribution. EBSCO and ProQuest were beginning to consider offering collections of e-books for rental or purchase.

In the early '90s, the Charleston Conference was a family affair. I remember attendees and speakers bringing their children. There was one small "spat" about us allowing babies and small children, but we worked positively around it. It was part of the intimacy of the conference—the sense of a community gathering together. It was important for me to hold onto that sense of community as the conference continued to grow. Attendance had leaped up from twenty-five people in 1980, to over one hundred in 1986, to more than five hundred in 1997.

This growth occurred alongside changes in the city of Charleston itself. The I-526 extension had opened, which meant that the conference was able to accommodate more people in nearer hotels. In 1993, the James Island Connector had been completed, allowing more growth. In 1995, the Citadel admitted its first woman, Shannon Faulkner. This was a hard-fought and controversial move, since the Citadel had only admitted males in the past.

In 1995, the Arthur Ravenel Jr. Bridge was completed, allowing for more access for those who wanted to stay in less expensive hotels across the bridges!

About this time, my best friend, Cerise Oberman, moved away for a job in Minnesota. Cerise was an awesome friend. We had lots of fun together. I especially remember omelets at the Goody House! We had also published a book together: *Theories of Bibliographic Education: Designs for Teaching* (R. R. Bowker, 1982).

In 1999, the Charleston Conference began the vendor showcase. When I started the conference, I had two resolutions: no commerce or exhibits, and no concurrent sessions! Twenty years later, as the attendance at the conference expanded and topics were more diverse, I was to realize that more concurrent discussions were necessary to accommodate the demand for sessions. Here I have to state that my personal philosophy was, and even now continues to be, against limiting discussion sessions. However, cooler and saner minds than mine have pointed to the unwieldiness of too many concurrent sessions. Case closed.

In terms of exhibits, I came to see that all types of products, including commercial products, were a necessary part of the dialogue. As one attendee said, "The social events become part of the learning process." This was where exhibitors could display and promote their products and services. We had exhibitor booths during the showcase, and many of the freebies were everywhere. Charles Watkinson's teenage son, as well as many of us, remember them: the squishy stress ball, the plastic bottle opener, T-shirts, diaries, and all kinds and colors of notebooks and pens, mechanical pencils, thumb drives, candy, small notebooks, portable staplers, beachballs, sunspecs, and so on.

The year 2000 marked the twentieth anniversary of the conference. The theme was "Is Bigger Better?" We had a big celebration at the Charleston Visitor Center. I danced with Lyman Newlin, and we ate pieces of the vanilla and chocolate cake! It was also the first year of the Beastly Breakfasts (held on Saturday, November 4), when attendees could talk about issues in which they were interested.

2001: "The Trends They Are A'Changing." That was definitely true! Transformation in libraries and publishing seemed inevitable. Libraries and learning turned digital. Electronic publishing and open access joined conversations.

It wasn't just the conversations at the conference that were changing with the times; it was the conference itself and the attendees who were changing. The generational mix underlined the different roles of the speakers and participants, which had been the point of mixing librarians, publishers, vendors, and consultants together. EBSCO and ProQuest were marketing e-books on their platforms.

2002: "Two Faces Have I: One for Books and One for Bytes." There was definitely strategic change in libraries and publishing. Information was no longer scarce but superabundant. Serials, magazines, works appearing in parts as opposed to books, long-written or printed compositions were prevalent.

2003: "Games People Play." Were people getting their sea legs? We had always been distinct groups, but we seemed to be getting new senses of humor and togetherness. Enter Heidi Hoerman to bring us even more together, with the first issue of "News From Yesterday."

2004: "All the World's a Serial." This is oh so true! The Charleston Conference began for books and serials when books were the dominant actor. Over the years, I have had more than one person suggest that I change the name of the conference. I refuse. To me, our name is our BRAND! Why (expletive deleted) mess with it?

That year, Lyman Newlin received the first Charleston Conference Lifetime Achievement Award. The first skit, "The Shock of Recognition," was performed. We had a skit every year for ten or so years. John Riley and Eleanor Cook and many other colleagues were the actors and driving forces behind these great skits!

2004 was also the year the conference used the Francis Marion Hotel for the first time—a decision that would turn out fabulously. The Francis Marion is historic, dating to 1923. At its origin, it advertised a radio in every room. "Goat Sammy," the model for Porgy from Gershwin's *Porgy and Bess*, sat in his goat cart on the corner selling peanut candy. Children would cry out "Charleston for a dime" and do the famous dance for tourists.

Initially, there were some complaints about the hotel being rundown, but those quickly vanished when attendees saw the other prices in town. Also, the aged charm of the place just grows on you. The Swamp Fox bar and the little restaurant are delightful, and somehow, they manage to accommodate most who want to crowd in.

In the years that followed, the Marion would always be welcoming, accommodating any request we made. No other hotel in town would match their graciousness. And for that I especially thank Gayle Karolczyk, Stephen Parker, and Steven Dopp. A Starbucks got added on the corner, and we all know how vital that is to the librarian psyche.

Outside the hotel is the other lucky element. Marion Square is a nice grassy sward with hotels around it. A farmers' market is held on Saturday morning with all kinds of food, including the legendary Southern boiled peanuts.

King and Calhoun Streets are the virtual crossroads of the city. College students bustle about, and the campus is a half block over. Citadel cadets in their uniforms can be seen at night. Up and down King Street are bars and restaurants of all variety and no street crime or derelicts.

Take a pleasant walk down King and you come to a strip of antique shops, then Broad Street and the one true historical part of the city. The blue of the harbor beckons.

Over the years, I've seen the town population balloon, but tourism has swelled astoundingly. Charleston now ranks with New Orleans as one of the most popular spots in the country. Bachelorette parties and destination weddings are a thing.

Along with the rise of residents and tourism came the multiplication of restaurants. The choices are overwhelming, and they're all within walking distance of the grand old hotel—may it live forever.

My favorites came and went, and some stayed. The Francis Willard in the Market had great ribs and an electric train that ran around on an overhead track, which enthralled our young son.

The Old Town had a Greek blue front, chickens turning on spits, and the great Steve's Special with gyro meat, shrimp, chicken, fish, and potatoes. Wuf.

There was a French restaurant, briefly, that served a shrimp Provençal to die for. The owner chef was French and didn't believe in paying taxes. When his arrears caught up with him, he fled the country. Today, French cuisine is admirably served by Rue de Jean, which is a model of a Paris bistro inside.

The Mills Hotel has a great restaurant where my husband and I would celebrate our anniversary with steak Diane and Caesar salad prepared at the table. The Fulton Five has a fabulous bar with dry martinis, where Charles Watkinson and the University of Michigan launched Lolly Gasaway's book of copyright columns from *Against the Grain*.

The conference truly took on a special magic, and I had little to do with it. All emanated from a piece of vibrant geography where I ended up due to my husband's job. When I look at the alternative places we might have gone, I know I could not have pulled this off. None of them have the corner of King and Calhoun with a grand hotel with soul.

The year after we moved into the Francis Marion, 2005, marked the conference's twenty-fifth anniversary. With 192 speakers in 88 sessions, we expanded into a second hotel, using the Embassy Suites in addition to the Francis Marion.

More epigrams from Gilbert and Sullivan: "Things Are Seldom What They Seem, Skim milk masquerades as cream." Who is to know where all this change is taking us? Still, believe in stability amid all this change.

That was also the year I was appointed to the IMLS board. The Institute of Museum and Library Services, an independent federal agency, was established in 2006 and is the main source of federal support for museums and libraries within the United States.[5] The advisory board includes twenty-four members who advise the agency on general policies with respect to the duties, power, and authorities of IMLS. I was initially nominated by Robert S. Martin, director of IMLS (2001–2005) and professor and director of the School of Library and Information Studies at the Texas Women's University. Later in the lengthy process, I was confirmed by US Supreme Court Justice Sandra Day O'Connor, nominated by President George W. Bush, and confirmed by the US Senate.

I was only on the IMLS board for a little over five years, but it was incredibly instructive to meet the diverse board members and hear their challenges, desires, and opportunities. I consider it a real honor to have served on the board, a hallmark of stability and equilibrium amid all these changes to our museums and libraries.

Conclusion

But during 1990–2005, look at all that took place! There were several hundred benchmarks that would influence the future:

1995

- First Charleston Conference concurrent sessions at its fifteenth anniversary.

1996

- May 1: The Internet Archive and the Wayback Machine were founded by Brewster Kahle; free repositories of webpages.
- The International Coalition of Library Consortia (ICOLC), a group of academic consortium leaders, began to meet.

1997

- Journal conversations between libraries and publishers shifted from print to online; comments: Charleston better at being civil than ALA.
- Music approval plans began to appear.
- March 12: Science Direct (Elsevier) was launched, beginning adversarial relations between libraries and publishers.
- Rick Anderson (early in his career) at the Conference delivered a plenary conference paper against library service fees;

John Berry, the editor of Library Journal was in the audience. There was much discussion!

1998

- Google was created by Sergei Brin and Larry Page.

1999

- The first Charleston vendor showcase started bringing commercial companies into the conversations as well as many innovative new products.

2000

- Searching the web started; copyright: cyberspace.
- The "Big Deal" was discussed by Rick Anderson et al.; tension led to the open access conversation.
- Publishers began to digitize backfiles.
- SPARC kept track of Big Deal cancellations; Big Deal dissipated and moved into transformative agreements, but many had the opinion that transformative agreements were no more sustainable than the Big Deal (Rick Anderson); was it a mechanism for broadening open access?

2004

- Google went public.
- Elsevier launched Scopus.
- February 4: Facebook for Harvard students.

2005

- Charleston Conference spans five days, 950 registrants, 130 planned sessions and activities, nine preconferences, and more; $325 registration fee.
- Leah's first conference as a worker; Wyatt (Caroline Goldsmith's son) is less than a year old and wears Regina Semko's "Ask me" button.
- Google bought Android for $50 million.

Humble beginnings. Rivers Dormitory Hall at College of Charleston, site of the first conference meeting. Exterior (above) and interior (below).

Off to a good start. Brian Cox and Katina Strauch at a conference beer-tasting event (above). Dancing and drinking have been essential to the conference since the start (below).

Various conference attendees. Photos from the 25th anniversary Memory Book. Note to Readers: Can you identify other familiar faces? If so, let Katina or Leah know. Top left, red tie: Joe Bolchoz (College of Charleston); top right: Judy Luther, Anne and Ken Robichaux; center: Katina and Lyman Newlin; bottom left: Deanna Astle, Jerry Curtis.

Top left: Katina and Judy Webster; top right: Bobbie Carlson, Barbara Homes-Stewart; bottom right: Dorinda Harmon, Corrie Marsh, Sandy Paul.

Top left: Bobbie Carlson, Barbara Homes-Stewart; top right: Steve Danes and his wife; bottom right: Sonya Killian, Lyman Newlin.

Top left: Audrey Melkin, Norm Demarais; top right: Katina at a book signing event; bottom left: Chuck Hamaker at podium; bottom right: Porter's Gate at the College of Charleston.

Top left: The old Cooper River Bridges in Charleston; top right: Katina and Chuck Hamaker; bottom left and right: conference attendees in the Carolina Ballroom at the Francis Marion Hotel.

Top left: Rick Anderson and T. Scott Plutchak (seated), Anthony Watkinson (standing); top right: Tony Ferguson; bottom left: conference attendees in the lobby of the Francis Marion Hotel; bottom right: Rick Anderson and T. Scott Plutchak.

Top left: Katina ringing the bell to call the session to order; top right: Derek Law; bottom left and right: Charleston Conference Skit Players.

Top photos: Charleston Conference Skit Players; bottom center:
Michael Stevens; bottom right: R. David Lankes.

Pat Hawkins (left) and Caroline
Goldsmith in the Francis
Marion Hotel.

Toni Nix (left) and daughter,
Dana, at the conference reception on board the USS Yorktown.

Registration desk staff in the Francis Marion Hotel.

Lars Meyer (left) and Katina Strauch at an early Charleston vendor showcase.

Don Hawkins, conference blogger (left), and wife, Pat, information desk staff member.

Katina Strauch in her balcony suite overlooking the stage in the Performance Hall at the Gaillard Center.

Long Arm of the Law panelists: Ann Okerson, Bill Hannay, Kenneth Crews, and Ruth Okediji (left to right).

Richard Gallagher (left), Katina Strauch (center), and Leah Hinds (right) at the opening keynote of the 2023 conference for the announcement of the acquisition by *Annual Reviews*.

Portrait of Mario Casalini, painted by Bruce Strauch.

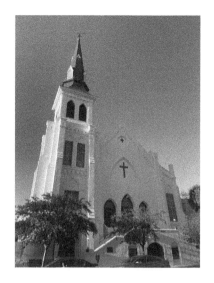

Francis Marion Hotel, headquarters location for the conference.

Emanuel African Methodist Episcopal Church, AKA Mother Emanuel, site of the horrific 2015 shooting.

The Charleston Gaillard Center, the expanded venue.

Katina Strauch at her home on Sullivan's Island, 2024.

Part 3

2006–2023: What's Past is Prologue

Chapter 7

THE FORMATIVE YEARS

Hooray for the Gaillard Center!

I guess it was around 2010 that we heard rumors of a meeting between Joe Riley and Martha Ingram about the Gaillard Center. We were happy with the Francis Marion Hotel as a meeting site, but we decided to have meetings with other larger venues as the Charleston Conference grew. I was curious about the Omni Hotel in Charleston and decided to pay them a visit. Sharna Williams came with me. Back then the Omni was the up-and-coming hotel. It had many sleeping and meeting rooms that were well-appointed and could accommodate our group comfortably. We met with several hotel employees, many women who were from "off" as I recall. The tour of the sleeping and meeting rooms was excellent. However, the hotel wanted us to book and guarantee payment for a minimum number of sleeping rooms at a fixed price which was quite high. I did not think that we could get attendees to come and pay those fees and neither did Sharna. We started looking around elsewhere. Back then, Charleston was growing. The Greek restaurant on the corner served mouth-watering dishes. I hoped that the hotel would be more flexible, but that did not happen.

There was a sales rep at the Embassy Suites, which was nearby. He was much more accommodating and willing to make a deal, but they had fewer sleeping rooms and not nearly as many meeting rooms. You may remember that the Embassy Suites was the site of the old Citadel's campus, so I was hoping for an agreeable outcome. I talked to the Embassy for many years until the aggressive sales rep moved on. The Embassy deal was tied up with the Hampton Inn, which was nearby and had a swimming pool. We secured sleeping room blocks at both the Embassy and the Hampton Inn, but never for a meeting.

Next up was the Courtyard by Marriott, which was being constructed on Meeting and Calhoun where the old Holiday Inn had been. The Courtyard had a fantastically aggressive and creative sales rep, Polly Ann Elliott, who I still miss, but she moved on about five years ago. The Marriott has many hotels in Charleston where we still have room blocks, but they did not have the number of meeting rooms that we required. There is a Marriott near the Citadel that has several meeting rooms, which we were interested in using for smaller meetings.

But for sure, the Charleston Conference was quite lucky when Martha Rivers Ingram and Charleston mayor Joe Riley agreed that the City of Charleston needed a world-class cultural institution to elevate the artistic community. They proposed splitting the $142 million cost of

construction fifty-fifty between the city and local philan-
thropists. Construction began in August 2012 and was
completed in October 2015 on the new Gaillard Center,
which included the 1,818-seat Martha and John M. Rivers
Performance Hall.[1]

PS: There is meeting space in North Charleston that
I was urged to consider, but I am committed to having the
Charleston Conference in downtown Charleston. Hooray
for the Gaillard Center!

Riding the Waves of Change

This was a period of upheaval in the library and scholarly
publishing world: we faced tough economic times, budget
cuts, furloughs, and the cancellation of some resources (as
highlighted by the 2009 conference theme: "Necessity Is
the Mother of Invention"). Scholarly publishing was continuing to transform, with the move to open access continuing apace. Big publishers were coming onboard, while
some researchers were reluctant to share data, as discussed
in the 2011 conference keynote by Mackenzie Smith (MIT),
"Data Papers in the Network Era."[2]

In 2010, Jeffrey Beall sounded the alarm about predatory
journals in a noteworthy article published in *The Charleston
Advisor*. This became a big part of the conversation.

We were wrestling with questions about discovery
and delivery. By 2010/11, libraries were buying their first

e-books, shifting the focus to cost per use and university presses. In 2015, the Charlotte Initiative on eBook Principles advanced the principles of unlimited simultaneous users, no digital rights management (DRM), irrevocable perpetual access, and archival rights.

The conference brought the community together in a lively conversation about these changes and challenges. In 2010, there was debate around altmetrics and the shift in the conversation from book acquisitions to scholarly communication. In 2014, Lisa Hinchliffe delivered a presentation, "Happiness is Library Automation," advancing the idea that discovery should be delivery.[3] In 2012, Annette Thomas, the CEO of Macmillan, delivered her landmark presentation about "building from the user back," highlighting a user-centered approach.[4] At the 2019 conference, Brewster Kahle announced a major new initiative from the Internet Archive and Better World Books rooted in Kahle's concern about the increase in misinformation online; his strategy was to enhance and encourage deeper exploration of credible online sources of information such as Wikipedia.[5]

Through this period of change, the library community found new ways to stay connected and exchange ideas. The conference remained an important part of this project of community building; it grew and evolved, but always retained its unique spirit. We added concurrent sessions, providing speaking slots for the librarians who need them. Conference organizers added the first-timers cocktail party and began outreach to students and junior members. It was a challenge, sometimes, to keep everyone connected (literally—the Wi-Fi struggled to keep up, as everyone logged in with multiple devices!). But we made it work.

Thirty Years—We are Family!

In 2010, the conference celebrated its thirtieth anniversary; there were 360 speakers in 159 plenary and concurrent sessions, and 1,188 registrants. Conferencegoers enjoyed the "Anything Goes" parody written by Greg Tananbaum and performed by Jack Montgomery, and a skit featuring participants dancing up the aisles in feather boas, singing "We Are Family."

In addition to building the conference, I continued to advance professionally in other ways: Around 2013, my former library school professor called me up and told me he was nominating me for appointment to the UNC-Chapel Hill Board of Visitors. This became a springboard for various opportunities: one of the board members was potentially interested in purchasing *Against the Grain*, and some potential buyers for the conference continued to approach me.

Remembering Mother Emanuel and Cynthia Graham Hurd

I remember vividly the ghastly shooting at the Mother Emanuel African Methodist Episcopal Church on June 17, 2015. I was working in my office at the College of

Charleston Library and looking over a cart of books to find reviews to decide whether we should keep them or not. In several cases, I was asking the department selector what he or she recommended. We were interrupted by an urgent news flash. There had been a shooting down the street at the Mother Emanuel Church, but news was scarce. I knew that the church was only a stone's throw from the College of Charleston campus. For several hours, we were instructed to stay safe, since we didn't know anything about the shooter or what might happen next. There was a lot of concern and general stress. We did learn that the shooting had taken place during a Bible study class at the Church, which was even more horrifying. Several days later, we learned that nine people had been killed, including the senior pastor, State Senator Clementa Pinckney. All ten victims were African American. It was the deadliest mass shooting at a place of worship in US history.

We did know that Cynthia Graham Hurd, a librarian and community leader in Charleston, was one of the victims. She was only fifty-four, one of six children. She graduated from Clark Atlanta University in 1982 with a degree in mathematics. She got her library degree in 1989 from the University of South Carolina. She had worked as a librarian in the SC library system for thirty-one years. There have been several honors and a Cynthia Graham Hurd Foundation established in her memory. In 2015, the Charleston County Public Library renamed the St. Andrews Regional Library, and a mural was painted in her honor.

Every year at the Charleston Library Conference there is a presentation and award in Cynthia Graham Hurd's name given by Springer Nature. Long may we remember her.

A New Era

In 2016, I retired from my position at the College of Charleston Addlestone Library. It was an emotional event, remembering thirty-seven years of memories. The library gave me a huge all-day reception with my colleagues reminiscing. A few tears were shed. And now here I am, writing a memoir of my career published by Against the Grain Press through the University of Michigan Fulcrum platform. But I haven't retired from the Charleston Conference! No siree!

AND WAIT!!! By December 27, 2019, COVID-19 was beginning to appear in the news! A huge threat, according to the CDC. The conference directors turned to Leah and me to respond to questions from attendees. Leah and I decided to pivot and have a virtual event instead. Actually, it turned out that the virtual event worked nicely! The conference reemerged as an in-person event in 2021, carrying forward hybrid elements.

Realizing the clock was ticking, I finally decided the time was right to sell my babies *ATG* and the conference. In 2022, I received several bids; the best was from Annual Reviews (AR). This is when Richard Gallagher started talking to me about the conference, following the sale of

The Charleston Advisor. Jonathan Michael, their wonderful CFO, was also involved. The sale to AR was finalized in 2023. I was relieved, and I believe that AR, a nonprofit publisher whose mission is to synthesize and integrate knowledge for the benefit of society and the progress of science, is the perfect choice. After many bids, conversations, and discussions, I'm gratified that the forward-looking Richard Gallagher and AR will continue the legacy of the Charleston Hub.

I've also been honored to meet and connect with a lot of friends and retirees who continued to come to the Charleston Conference. Hopefully AR will add a special fee for retirees. This will help the conference remain a place where we can look back even as we look forward, connect with old friends while looking toward the future, and imagine what there still is to learn.

Chapter 8

MORE OPPORTUNITIES

What were conference attendees talking about during those years?

There's no way to cover the breadth and depth of conversations that took place over all the years, but here's a sampling of some of the important hot topics during this time period.

2010–2011

- Many libraries were buying their first e-books.
- First aquarium reception, easy to have conversations.
- Plenary presentations from:

  Rick Anderson, University of Utah, titled "Let Them Eat... Everything: Embracing a Patron-Driven Future"[1]

  "Creating a Trillion-Field Catalog: Metadata in Google Books," from Jon Orwant, Google Books Engineering Manager[2]

  "The Semantic Web," by Michael Keller, Stanford University[3]

"The DPLA and Its Implementation," by Robert Darnton, Harvard University; Rachel Frick, Digital Public Library of America; and Sanford Thatcher, Penn State University Press Director Emeritus[4]

"The Future of Online Newspapers," by Deborah Cheney, Penn State University Library; Chris Cowan, ProQuest; Chuck Palsho, NewsBank; and Frederick Zarndt, Global Connections.[5]

- First "Long Arm of the Law" panel with Bill Hannay, "the Singing Lawyer," on the Google Books, SkyRiver, and Georgia State e-reserves cases.[6]

2012–2013

- Conversation changed; more people started coming to presentations, and discussion is more about discovery/technology than which book you need; we aren't sure we need books anymore!
- Extraordinary that one-third of the attendees are first-timers every year; maybe sending junior staff to learn about acquisitions, people of different generations who are new to the profession, values about community-centered scholarship.
- Diversity is a throughline, not stuck in a graying crowd.
- Plenary highlights include: the landmark presentation "Our New Job Description" by Annette Thomas (CEO of Macmillan), enabling technology on what users need, not what

librarians think it should be;[7] Anurag Acharya, Google Scholar, on "Integrating Discovery and Access for Scholarly Articles";[8] "SCOAP[3]: Going Live with the Dream," by Ann Okerson (celebrating its tenth anniversary at the 2024 Charleston Conference!).[9]

2014

- ProQuest and Ex Libris merge, bringing together different organizational cultures (ProQuest female, Ex Libris male— different social conversations (hunting)).
- Enter cost per use and university presses to the conversation.
- Cost per use versus public good.
- In Charleston, people become human because you can see them (publishers and librarians)—more alike, people looking outwards, NIHITO (nothing interesting happens in the office).
- Input from the front lines, how to present open access to professors.
- Senior people can get too cliquey—conversations at the fringes.

Chapter 9

And now for something a little different! I asked industry expert Darrell W. Gunter, founder and owner of Gunter Media Group, Inc., to contribute a section on the advances in publishing technology that took place over the formative years of the conference.

SCHOLARLY PUBLISHING INDUSTRY DEVELOPMENTS BY DARRELL W. GUNTER

CD-ROM Technology

The introduction of CD-ROM technology in libraries began in the late 1980s and early 1990s. This period saw significant developments in how libraries managed and provided access to information.

The early adoption of CD-ROM technology in libraries can be traced back to initiatives such as those by the American Association for the Advancement of Science (AAAS), which provided databases to university libraries. By 1990, the implications and considerations of implementing CD-ROM workstations were being discussed extensively, indicating the growing interest and usage of this technology in library settings.[1]

By 1993, the University of Dar es Salaam (UDSM) library in Tanzania had also started incorporating

CD-ROM technology into its services, reflecting a broader trend of adoption across different regions and types of libraries.[2]

For more detailed information, you can refer to the studies and articles on the subject, such as those available through the National Academies Press and Emerald Insight, and elsewhere.[3]

Start and Developments of Scholarly Publishing Consortia

The concept of consortia in scholarly publishing has been around for several decades, with notable developments accelerating in the late twentieth and early twenty-first centuries. One of the significant early initiatives was the Scholarly Publishing and Academic Resources Coalition (SPARC), founded in 1998.[4] SPARC was established to address issues related to the high cost of scholarly journals and to promote open access publishing. Its primary aim was to create partnerships and collaborations to improve access to academic resources.

Key Developments

TRANSFORMATIVE AGREEMENTS

Transformative agreements have been a significant development in the landscape of scholarly publishing consortia.

These agreements, often between publishers and library consortia, aim to shift from subscription-based models to open access models. Examples include the "Read-and-Publish" and "Publish-and-Read" agreements that bundle payments for reading and publishing into a single contract, facilitating a smoother transition to open access.[5]

LIBRARY PUBLISHING COALITION (LPC)

Established in 2014, the LPC is a community-led membership association comprising academic and research libraries and library consortia.[6] The LPC supports the creation, dissemination, and curation of scholarly works and promotes library publishing as a means to advance scholarly communication.

GLOBAL EXPANSION AND COLLABORATION

Over the years, the scope of consortia has expanded globally. Initiatives like the European Open Science Cloud (EOSC) and cOAlition S have emerged, promoting open access and collaborative research infrastructures across Europe and beyond. These consortia facilitate data sharing, resource pooling, and collaborative research efforts, enhancing the accessibility and impact of scholarly publications.

ONE NATION, ONE SUBSCRIPTION POLICY

Some countries, such as India, are exploring national-level subscription policies to ensure comprehensive access to scholarly resources. This approach aims to negotiate country-wide access to academic journals and publications, thereby reducing costs and increasing accessibility for researchers and institutions nationwide.[7]

These developments highlight the evolving nature of scholarly publishing consortia, focusing on collaboration, cost-efficiency, and enhanced access to academic resources. Consortia continue to play a crucial role in navigating the transition toward open access and addressing the challenges posed by traditional subscription models.

For further details, you can refer to resources such as the Scholarly Kitchen and SPARC websites.

Chronological Developments in the Scholarly Publishing Industry

Early Developments (Pre-2000)

The emergence of digital technologies and the World Wide Web in the 1990s began transforming scholarly publishing. The Budapest Open Access Initiative in 2002 was a significant milestone that defined open access as making scientific literature freely available online without charge.

THE UNIVERSITY LICENSING PROGRAM (TULIP)

The TULIP project was a significant initiative by Elsevier Science Publishers, aimed at exploring the electronic distribution of scholarly journals. This project, which ran from 1991 to 1995, was spearheaded by Karen Hunter, a key figure at Elsevier.

The primary objectives of the TULIP project were:

- To test systems for networked delivery of scientific journals.
- To understand the impact of electronic distribution on libraries and end users.
- To explore the technical and operational issues related to such a distribution model.

The project involved the digitization of forty-two materials science journals, which were then delivered to nine participating universities in the United States. These universities included prominent institutions like the University of Michigan and Carnegie Mellon University. The journals were provided in TIFF bitmapped page images and ASCII full-text format, which allowed for comprehensive testing of electronic access and usage.

The final report on the TULIP project, edited by Karen Hunter, indicated that the project was successful in demonstrating the feasibility and potential benefits of electronic journal distribution. It highlighted several key findings:

- Libraries and users were generally positive about the accessibility and convenience of electronic formats.
- Technical challenges related to data formats, network delivery, and user interfaces were identified and addressed.

The project paved the way for subsequent developments in digital libraries and electronic publishing, influencing future initiatives such as ScienceDirect.[8] The TULIP project is considered a pioneering effort in the transition from print to digital scholarly communication, and it set the stage for modern digital libraries and electronic journal platforms.

For more detailed information on the TULIP project and its outcomes, you can refer to the final report edited by Karen Hunter.[9]

From 1996, CD-ROM technology started being integrated into libraries, providing new ways to access and store scholarly materials.

2000–2010

The RoweCom Debacle

The RoweCom debacle in the early 2000s was a significant crisis in the library subscription industry. RoweCom, also known as Divine Information Services, was a subscription agent that managed journal subscriptions for libraries. The company faced severe financial issues, leading to its bankruptcy in January 2003.

RoweCom's parent company, Divine, Inc., allegedly transferred $73.7 million from RoweCom, leaving the company unable to fulfill prepaid subscription orders.[10] This financial mismanagement left over one thousand research institutions and libraries with a combined loss of at least $73.7 million.[11] Libraries that had relied on RoweCom for handling their journal subscriptions found themselves without the resources they had paid for, severely impacting their access to scholarly materials.[12]

In response to this crisis, the American Library Association (ALA) stepped in to mitigate the losses. The ALA signed an agreement with EBSCO Industries to continue the subscriptions for affected libraries.[13] EBSCO acquired RoweCom's US operations and worked with publishers to ensure that subscriptions were fulfilled despite the bankruptcy.

This event highlighted the vulnerabilities in the subscription management industry and prompted many libraries to reconsider their reliance on third-party agents for journal subscriptions. It also underscored the importance of having contingency plans and diversifying access to electronic resources.

2005–2014

The SEEDS Blog

The SEEDS blog, associated with the Society for Scholarly Publishing (SSP), launched in October 2005. It was a platform for early-career professionals in the scholarly publishing industry to share insights, experiences, and industry news. The blog served as a valuable resource for individuals new to the field, fostering a sense of community and providing guidance on various aspects of scholarly publishing.

However, the SEEDS blog was discontinued in September 2014 as part of SSP's strategic realignment of its digital communication efforts. This shift included a greater focus on other platforms and initiatives, such as the Scholarly Kitchen, which continues to provide extensive industry commentary and insights.

For more detailed information on the SEEDS blog and its history, you can refer to sources from the SSP and related archives.

2008

The Scholarly Kitchen

The Scholarly Kitchen was launched in February 2008.[14] It was established by the SSP to keep members and other interested parties aware of new developments in the scholarly publishing industry.

Open Access

The first open access journal was *Psycoloquy*, which was established in 1989 by Stevan Harnad. It was an early experiment in electronic publishing and served as a precursor to the open access movement.[15] This journal was published by the American Psychological Association and provided a platform for peer-reviewed articles in psychology and related fields, making them freely available online.[16]

Psycoloquy was significant in demonstrating the feasibility and benefits of open access, setting the stage for later developments in the open access publishing landscape, including initiatives like the Public Library of Science (PLOS) and BioMed Central (BMC) in the early 2000s.[17]

Commercial Agreements

- **2001**: The "Big Deal" subscription models became prevalent, offering bundled journal subscriptions to libraries, which led to increased costs and financial strain on library budgets.
- **2002**: Introduction of article processing charges (APCs) by open access publishers such as BioMed Central and PLOS, allowing authors to pay for the publication to make their work freely available.
- **Mid-2000s**: Growth of repositories for self-archiving (green open access) and increasing support for open access mandates by research funders and institutions.

2010–2015

- **Early 2010s**: Major academic publishers, including Elsevier, Springer, and Wiley, started embracing open access models, leading to a hybrid system where some articles in subscription journals were available open access.

- **2013**: The United States and several European countries began mandating open access for publicly funded research, significantly increasing the number of open access publications.
- **2015**: Formation of the Directory of Open Access Journals (DOAJ), which became a critical resource for identifying reputable open access journals.

2015–2020

- **2015–2018**: Analysis showed significant APC revenues for major publishers, highlighting the commercial success of the open access model for these companies.[18, 19]
- **2018**: Launch of cOAlition S and Plan S, aiming for full and immediate open access to scholarly publications funded by public grants.
- **Late 2010s**: Increased focus on combating predatory publishing practices and improving the quality and transparency of open access journals.

2020–Present

- **2022**: A memo from the US White House Office of Science and Technology Policy mandated that all federally funded research be published with green or gold open access by 2026.

- **2023**: Reports emphasize the need for strategic planning in scholarly communication infrastructure, highlighting the importance of sustainable and shared digital infrastructure to support open access and long-term preservation of scholarly works.[20]

These developments illustrate the rapid evolution of scholarly publishing from traditional subscription models to diverse open access frameworks, driven by digital advancements, economic pressures, and policy mandates.

Launch and Updates of Plan S

Plan S was launched in September 2018 by cOAlition S, a consortium of national research agencies and funders from twelve European countries. The initiative aimed to make all scientific publications resulting from publicly funded research freely available by 2021. The primary goal was to ensure that scientific outputs were accessible without barriers, promoting the principle that "no science should be locked behind paywalls".[21]

Key Components of Plan S

- **Immediate open access**: Researchers must publish in compliant open access journals or platforms.

- **Funding**: APCs are covered by funders or institutions, not researchers.
- **Copyright retention**: Authors retain copyright under an open license, such as Creative Commons.
- **Transparency**: Transparent pricing and business models for open access publishing.

Updates on Plan S

- **2020 implementation**: By the end of 2020, Plan S mandated that researchers receiving grants from coalition funders must publish their findings in open access journals or platforms.[22] This move prompted several publishers to adapt their policies to comply with Plan S requirements.
- **Transformative Journals**: Springer Nature and other publishers introduced "transformative journals," which are hybrid journals committed to transitioning to full open access over time. These journals report on their progress annually to ensure compliance with Plan S goals.[23]
- **Support and Compliance**: As of 2023, Plan S has seen broad support from various institutions and publishers globally. However, challenges remain in ensuring compliance across different regions and adapting to specific local contexts.

Plan S continues to shape the landscape of scientific publishing, pushing for greater transparency and accessibility in how research findings are disseminated. For further details on the latest developments, you can refer to sources such as Springer Nature and the official Plan S website.

The Advent of COVID and AI

The Frankfurt Bookfair experienced a high 7,500 exhibitors in 2018, only to become a virtual meeting in 2020 due to COVID and rebound to 4,200 exhibitors in 2023. Hall 4.2 was the main hall for scientific, technical, and medical (STM) publishers, but due to the reduced exhibitors, the STM publishers were moved to hall 4.0 in 2022.

2018

- Visitors: Around 285,024.
- Exhibitors: Approximately 7,503 from 109 countries.

2019

- Visitors: Around 302,267.
- Exhibitors: Approximately 7,450 from 104 countries.

2020

- Visitors: Due to the COVID-19 pandemic, the physical fair was canceled, and a virtual event was held. The virtual event attracted over 200,000 unique users online.
- Exhibitors: No physical exhibitors; virtual participation took place.

2021

- Visitors: Around 73,500 (reduced due to ongoing pandemic restrictions).
- Exhibitors: Approximately 2,013 exhibitors from 80 countries (smaller scale due to the pandemic).

2022

- Visitors: Around 180,000.
- Exhibitors: Approximately 4,000 from 95 countries (gradual recovery after the pandemic).

2023

- Visitors: Around 182,000.
- Exhibitors: Approximately 4,200 from over 100 countries (continued recovery post-pandemic).

The numbers for 2023 show a trend of gradual recovery following the pandemic-impacted years, although the figures have not yet returned to pre-pandemic levels.

Publishers had to conduct business in this new virtual world and have slowly regained their in-person meetings with their customers. We can expect for this new blended business of virtual and in person to continue as the role of the knowledge worker will become more prevalent.

Generative Artificial Intelligence

In June of 2021, my edited volume, *Transforming Scholarly Research with Blockchain Technologies*, was published by IGI Global. The edited volume became a best seller for IGI. ChatGPT was launched in November 2022 and quickly built a significant user base for the free service. They launched the paid 4.0 service shortly thereafter.

The scholarly publishing industry is currently in development mode for generative artificial intelligence (AI) services.

Gadget Software's TopicLake Insights is a new AI-driven knowledge system. It takes static documents and transforms them into a dynamic, interconnected web of information. AI-generated metadata serves as the key to understanding, navigating, and expanding this network. Unlike static archives, TopicLake Insights constantly evolves as it ingests new data, creating a system that grows and adapts in real time.

THE ROLE OF AI

AI breaks down complex documents into distinct topics, summaries, and semantic annotations. This disaggregation process allows for more granular insights and a richer understanding of the document's content. Metadata is generated contextually, meaning the AI understands the relationships between topics and ideas, which it encodes into the metadata for more intelligent navigation.

REAL-TIME EVOLUTION

Unlike traditional systems where metadata is static, TopicLake Insights updates and refines its metadata as new information is added. This allows for a flexible and scalable repository of information that reflects the most up-to-date insights, critical for handling ongoing changes in policies, laws, and regulations. This service and other AI services will certainly change how information is researched, cited, published, and consumed.

Back to Katina!

Thank you, Darrell, for this excellent history!

Part 4

2024 and Beyond (The Importance of Being Earnest)

"Map out the future but do it in pencil."
—Jon Bon Jovi

Chapter 10

THE BIG PICTURE

It's been a grand forty-five years. I got out of a narrow library environment and met the great and good of the entire industry. I've been around the world, seen the stacks of the Bodleian, the twice-burned library of Leuven, and the forbidden card catalog of the Russian National. And I've seen time and tide sweep the industry.

Whither academic libraries? At the origin of my career, college was lectures with a library of books and journals to provide supplemental research reading. Students wrote down pearls of wisdom in notebooks and imagined themselves fully educated, little grasping all that was not said in class because there wasn't enough time.

In the '60s, college administrators hit upon publish-or-perish as a fine method to control faculty and flex their own power. Publishing requirements for all faculty, at even the smallest of colleges, became a requirement. This initiated a scramble to purchase as much material in the library as possible for use in research. And multiple new journals sprang up to serve the universe of faculty. A lot of footnoted minutiae got added to the data heap.

By the '90s, electronic journals appeared. This briefly gave the illusion of providing limitless data for the library user. Everyone saw the future as moving toward positive ends.

And then came Google. With its search engines churning away 24/7, the knowledge data exploded beyond any previously conceived proportions.

Librarians rocked along with changing times, changing cataloging methods and resenting that all knowledge wasn't free.

The professorial lectures sometimes became politicized, and this led to public resentment over funding and decreased enrollment. Almost anyone but an administrator could look at tuition and enrollment trends and see the college system we began with soon would be dying a hard death.

College will be reborn. It is purely a matter of adjusting curriculum and tuition. It will be wrenching for those making the current big salaries, but it will happen.

What about the clouds of data? How will data be organized?

Interlibrary loan became important when faculty were all required to publish and were desperate to get research materials that simply could not be held in their library collection. Electronic journals have largely moderated this need. The small activity in this area will no doubt be a matter of interpreting intellectual property rights.

You have to be able to find what you want to get. Cataloging puts data in a structure you understand to access it. Historically, every library had a catalog department with librarians picking at decimal points and headings.

OCLC appeared in 1971 online as a novel solution. One central cataloging service. You had to pay to join, and catalogers sometimes disputed the OCLC cataloging records as too many different librarians created them.

Next came Henriette Avram, a computer programmer and systems analyst who developed MARC, the international data standard that opened up the basis for library cooperation and automation. Bibliographic records were dispatched on magnetic tape to libraries around the country, and in 1971 MARC became the standard for electronic cataloging. Avram performed a daunting task. The library catalog contained millions of items—books, maps, films, sound recordings, and much more, in hundreds of languages, many using non-Roman alphabets. The cards for each item contained discrete pieces of information, each to be represented with a separate mathematical algorithm.[1] As it is now, libraries can edit and make other different MARC records. This complicates and increases the number of records in the OCLC database. This seems a waste of time and resources.

There will be fewer academic libraries as their duties will be renamed, absorbed, or swallowed up. Training and education for library work has evolved already, and library schools have attempted to adapt. However, technologies and innovation will continue, and library education and library schools must be merged with related emerging areas, renamed, or radically altered.

Everything that's being done is for some sort of benefit or profit. Open access is just an illusion. Companies are just trying to move the cost off to somewhere else.

What's Next?

Reading about all that has transpired in the past is humbling as well as inspiring. Obviously, no one knows what the future holds, but here are a few so-called "predictions" to start conversations.

- We must reduce the silo mindset. A silo is a closed way of organizing work into separate areas that are unable to communicate with other systems. Public services, technical services, and administration are silos, which can run the risk of not being able to communicate with other areas. A silo refers to the way grains are stored, assuring that the components can be kept separate. However, shifting trends and technology mean that silos can create barriers to collaboration across departments. Silos and the silo mindset must be broken down.
- End users deserve a place at the negotiation table. Who exactly are end users? The person or persons who uses or is intended to use a product. End users do not technically

or typically have the expertise of product designers, and, in fact, are usually overlooked, which may be the reason to seek their input.

- We must rethink our aversion to commerce and commercial companies. Great numbers of librarians bristle at the name "Elsevier," a noble company that has served the knowledge industry since 1880. Where does this aversion come from? Is it a matter of the definition of the word "profit"? Profit means coming out ahead. Does this always involve money? No. You can get a benefit from your experience, for example, or your involvement or participation in a nonprofit. Let's face it: commercial companies have the pocketbooks, personnel, and, yes, the interest in taking risks. AI and all the new tech that people are so enthused over are profit-motivated.
- Startups are everywhere and will become more dominant. It will depend on investment and confidence about the future. What's a startup? A newly established business or the process of setting something new in motion. It is in the first stage of operation, generally founded by one or several entrepreneurs who want to test a product or service for which they believe demand exists. Startups may frequently have the benefit of enthusiasm, youth, forward thinking, and probably some naivete. They also frequently do not reach their full potential by becoming successful.
- How important is technology as a partner? How do we define technology? Technology is the study of scientific knowledge in order to create tools and processes that can change the world. It is a capability given by the practical application of knowledge. It is broader than computer technology, meaning it is important in several other processes.

- Open access is a set of practices through which research outputs are distributed online, free of access charges or other barriers. There are numerous levels of open access (green, gold, hybrid, and others). These levels, as well as predatory publishing, have muddied the discovery layers enormously. Can librarians and scholarly publishers develop more robust discovery tools to make OA more viable?
- Libraries have been too passive when it comes to changing with the times, so the times changed them. Academic libraries will survive in some form, if only to train students to wend their way through the maze. Books and journals in the past have always been our go-to access tools. But as virtual tools and players—like ChatGPT and AI—emerge, books and journals must take a back seat.
- Cataloging/metadata will disappear/be replaced by AI developments.
- Interlibrary loan will disappear/be replaced by AI and OA.
- Libraries made little effort to organize the explosion of information, and now it's too overwhelming to even try.
- Both librarians and publishers have access to huge amounts of data which is organized differently. We must join forces to organize and use the data to our best advantages.
- Older, more mature librarians, publishers, vendors, and so on must be more respected as partners and must become more vocal. Let's talk.
- Artificial intelligence is the latest fad, but will it become a boondoggle—that is, give the appearance of adding more value than it is?

- The Global South will have a seat at the table. Like end users, the Global South has an important perspective that must be shared in and with the ecosystem.
- Consortia may break up or consolidate. Their goals must be shared and consolidated.
- Publishers and libraries share much in common. Rather than bumping heads in disagreement, they need to agree on possible ways to move forward.
- Finance will still be a necessary partner but will become part of operating expenses rather than a driving force.

Many of you will disagree with my predictions, and that's OK! I've had a grand time watching it all, and I am confident the sky's the limit as we reimagine libraries!! Thank you!

Profiles

These profiles do not include countless people who helped with the conference or the memoir. Katina is hoping to add to them. If you have a suggestion or ideas, please send them on!

The Core

These are the key people who keep *Against the Grain* and the Charleston Conference running day in and day out! Kudos all around!

Tom Gilson

I remember thirty to thirty-five years ago when Tom asked me if I wanted him to keep doing book reviews for *ATG*. Of course, I said "Yes!" At the time, Tom was head of reference services at the Robert Scott Small Library (later Addlestone). Tom has been working for *ATG* ever since.

His roles have expanded to include the Penthouse Suite interviews, general interviews (Tom asks great questions), and now the news and announcements and job postings. Tom is retired and has moved with his lovely wife, Carol, to a great house in Newberry, SC, with their dog and cat. Carol is a fabulous artist and teaches regular drawing classes. I love her paintings and have purchased several.

Caroline Goldsmith

How lucky I was when Leah's sister Caroline agreed to work for the Charleston Hub! Caroline worked as a paralegal for several years and has great technical editing skills. She also has two darling children, Wyatt and Addie. Caroline does a lot of the editing for *ATG*, the Charleston Briefings, the call for papers, and scoring for paper selection for the Charleston Conference and *ATG*. She also manages the conference sponsorships and off-site events. Thank goodness she works for the Charleston Hub.

Leah Hinds

What can I say? Leah, the exec director superwoman, does anything and everything that is needed to keep the Charleston Hub running. Leah was introduced to me by the ingenious Regina Semko, former conference registrar, back in 2004, when she worked at the College of

Charleston. Now she travels all over the globe to speak and represent the Hub. She manages the day-to-day operations for the Charleston Conference, *Against the Grain*, and a new publication named after yours truly, *Katina*, a part of Annual Reviews. Leah has two kids in college, and they both grew up coming to the conference each year. In fact, she started when her youngest was only a few months old! She loves animals and has a small farm with goats, chickens, mini pigs, and three dogs. I love hearing her rooster crow over the phone!

Matthew Ismail

I have known Matthew forever. He was working as a collection development librarian at Central Michigan University when he started writing articles and interviewing countless diverse people for *ATG* and the Charleston Hub podcasts. I credit Matthew with conceiving of and naming the Charleston Hub!

Toni Nix

Toni remembers when *ATG* was a little baby. I was looking for printers for *ATG* and went through—count—1-2-3-4 of them. A guy from the college was trying to help me find the right printer. We finally settled on Ashley Printing in West Ashley. As luck would have it, Toni Nix worked there.

It was 1992. Moving right along, there was staff turnover at Ashley Printing and a few deaths. Toni was only thirty-one. She quit working there in 1992 when the owner died. Toni knew more about printing than the owner, so I hired her to solve all my printing problems. She started working from home in 1997 and formed her LLC in 2002. And, boy, did she know what to do! I can't give enough praise to Toni! You wouldn't believe how much Toni has learned and picked up. She is very smart and very self-motivated! She is also loyal to her baby, *Against the Grain*!

Debbie Larsen

Debbie was the office manager at the Addlestone Library's main office. She went to secretarial school and learned all the necessary duties. She joined the Addlestone library staff when an earlier staff member quit. She is very positive and agreeable and always does what we need!

Sharna Williams

Sharna was working at the Charleston County Library as an LTA1. She was twenty-six when we hired her. She didn't have a degree but started pursuing one immediately. She was also single, and great friends with Shirley Davidson. It took a while for Sharna to get her confidence, but with Shirley's assistance, she got her bachelor's degree in English and became great friends with Caroline Hunt. Shirley introduced Sharna to Jerry Williams, who was working for the State Ports Authority, and whom she would marry approximately five years later. A great guy! I believe they will celebrate their thirtieth wedding anniversary this year.

Beth Bernhardt

Clever, inventive, and resourceful, Beth Bernhardt has kept the Charleston Conference program and speakers on track for the past twenty or so years! I believe her first time attending the conference was in 2001, and she started as a conference director around 2004. She remains the primary director in charge of it all! It was Rosann Bazirjian who assured me Beth would be the perfect director, and boy was she right! Beth was working at UNCG back then. When she told me she was moving to Oxford University Press, I was apprehensive, but I began to see this was the perfect move for her! Oh! And I forgot that Beth created the popular Trivia Night for the conference program! And another Oh! Beth persuaded her husband to help with A/V and as needed at the conference, even with all the refreshments during the reception on Thursday night! What a woman!!

Regina Semko

It's been thirty-five years since Regina Semko made her mark on the Charleston Conference, and the mark is indelible! Regina was working for the Lightsey Conference Center back then, when the powers that be made the decision to close the Center since they needed the space for classrooms and administrative use. I was happy with the management of the Lightsey, but they were relocating the staff. I asked Regina, the main staff member, to come work for the Conference. Regina had gotten a job with the CofC graduate school (where Leah was employed) and was incredibly industrious and artsy (she had been in charge of a group of volunteers who were running a local shop selling handmade items of all types). It was my good luck that Regina had this commercial experience. She knew the ins and outs of what the conference needed to get started. Regina went to meetings with college and hotel staff.

Sharna Williams still refers to notes of what Regina, nicknamed "Regenius," told her. In fact, Sharna tries to call Regenius every year or so. Regina retired several years ago to move to Youngstown, Ohio, with her mother, sisters, and brother. We still miss Regenius very much!!

Vignettes, Anecdotes, People

Richard Abel (1925–2013)

Richard Abel was a visionary innovator. He saw libraries buying identical titles from publishers. Why not make it easier to let libraries know what was available? He conceived of the approval plan, which would send cards with bibliographic information about the books, or the actual book itself. Libraries could preview the item and either buy it and pay, or return the book to the publisher. This would be beneficial to both the library and the publisher.

This idea was perfected by Blackwells and became very popular and no doubt lucrative for every organization involved. So the approval plan was born largely for academic libraries but continued and continues to expand.

Deanna Astle (1945–2005)

Deanna was wonderfully talented and creative. She loved to crochet colorful afghans and publish hard-hitting articles with Chuck Hamaker about differential serials pricing, dubbed the "serials crisis." I still treasure several of the afghans that she gave me. She was Chuck Hamaker's partner in exposing the differential serials pricing issues. Hamaker and Astle won the Bowker Ulrich's Serials Librarian of the Year Award in 1991 for their astute research articles on serials pricing by scholarly publishers of academic journals.

Besides knitting and crocheting, Deanna played the dulcimer delightfully, just like a pro.

Buzzy Basch (1934–2023)

He was always going to be alive! I never thought he would leave us! Buzzy was always ready to start a new serials business at the drop of a hat! He would travel all over the country (or even the world) to evaluate a potential business that he was interested in buying. He was always dressed colorfully in his unique sweaters. Buzzy loved to run preconferences or workshops for the Charleston Hub or any other venue. He was devoted to his long-time companion, Judy McQueen, and he would put aside serials business conversations to consider buying her magnificent jewelry. He attended every single Charleston Conference and Fiesole Retreat! He loved to walk everywhere, and he could walk you into the ground anywhere! I fondly remember him announcing at a retreat in Fiesole that he had just turned eighty. And that was at least ten years ago! I sure hope he can start serials businesses in heaven!

Rosann Bazirjian

Rosann is the hardest-workingest, sweetest conference coordinator that I have probably ever worked with. She was at Penn State when I first worked with her. Then she was appointed dean of libraries at UNC Greensboro. UNCG is a special place to me. I spent my first two college years as a student there. Last I heard, she had moved to Myrtle Beach.

John N. Berry (1933–2020)

Like most of you, I read John's editorials and opinion pieces for his almost fifty years working for *Library Journal*. I encountered him in person when we were both on the UNC-Chapel Hill Library School Advisory Board. He had an opinion on everything, and we didn't always agree, but that's OK. I remember one luncheon when he was talking about his army service where he held a clerk's job that allowed him to send people who annoyed him to the Korean War. A young woman at the table, suddenly screamed, "You killed my daddy!" The blood drained out of his face. In fact, she meant it in jest, and it was the most wicked and spontaneous one I've ever witnessed. Her father was still very much alive. We got no more information about John's army career. I think he had to go back to his room and lie down. My second encounter with John Berry was many years later when he called me panicked that he couldn't find his plane ticket. We had had a reception in my suite earlier and he hoped that he had left the plane ticket there. Yes! Whew!

Scott R. Bullard

Served as editor in chief of *Library Acquisitions: Practice and Theory* (*LAPT*). Scott was an early supporter and advocate of the Charleston Conference. He published the papers from the very early Charleston Conferences for several years until he resigned to work with textbook publisher associations. He had a great sense of humor and was the keynote of the very first independent acquisitions conference in St. Louis in 1990.

Mario Casalini (1926–1998)

Mario Casalini was the most urbane, elegant, cultured, courteous gentleman I have ever known. He always brought me gorgeous red roses.

He was known all over the world and even in the United States. As the Charleston Conference became more of a must-attend conference, he started coming regularly. One afternoon, he invited me and my husband to come to Fiesole, Italy. He was interested in the possibility of starting a Charleston-like conference in Italy. Italy was an awesome place and soon replaced Paris and Greece in our preferences. I remember landing in Fiesole late at night and we hadn't thought to get Italian money! But the Italians were wonderful and took us to the awesomely elegant Pensione Bencista across the way from the Casalini headquarters. Sadly, Mario died before the first retreat, but we planted an olive tree on the Casalini property, which lives on. The first

Fiesole Retreat was in 1999 and we have had a retreat every year for the past twenty-four years.[1]

I need to add that Michele Casalini, Mario's son, is now in charge of the Fiesole Retreats.

Pam Cenzer

My best friend of always, I met Pam when Mike Markwith introduced us at ALA many years ago. Susan Campbell was Pam's best friend and we all immediately bonded and still keep in touch. I have so many Pam and Susan stories! They each have a son and a daughter. Susan's daughter is an opera singer, and Pam's is an entomologist, and there's lots more to report! Congratulations to two very successful, now retired librarians!

Jake Chernofsky

Jacob L. ("Jake") Chernofsky retired from his position as editor and publisher of *AB Bookman's Weekly* magazine, which he joined in 1973. *AB*, which was originally titled *Antiquarian Bookman*, was founded on January 3, 1948, by Sol. Malkin, and the magazine's name was changed to *AB Bookman's Weekly* in 1967, "in recognition of a readership comprising mostly specialist dealers." *AB*, which had been widely read for several decades by people involved in the world of antiquarian books, suspended publication in December 1999.[2]

Eleanor Cook

I remember Eleanor asking me if she could come gratis to the Charleston Conference when she had just graduated from library school. Eleanor is always upbeat and enthusiastic, and I instantly liked her! She has worked long and hard at East Carolina University, and when she retired she took charge of the music library. Eleanor has supported the Charleston Conference from its very beginning. Her handsome husband Joe is a train enthusiast, which is way cool. Eleanor is always absorbed in some intriguing idea or project. She is also a really great guest!

Brian Cox

We have several pictures of Brian attending the Charleston Conference when he worked for Pergamon Press way back when. When I was young and ambitious (not to mention stupid), and I was in England, I tried to get an interview with the famous Robert Maxwell (though I had been briefed to expect negativity from many of his employees, like the incredible Della Sar and the doubly incredible Inge Valentine). Still, my philosophy is there's no chance of getting a positive answer if you don't try your best! So off I went to the splendiferous Headington Hill Hall hoping to meet the great Mr. Maxwell. Of course not, but I was lucky enough to be wined and dined by Brian Cox, plus I got a look inside the Maxwell Pergamon Press (later Elsevier) operation. I see that Brian has written a memoir and history of Pergamon. Haven't located it yet, but I will keep trying![3]

Martin Cummings

Entrepreneurially, Martin was interested in *The Charleston Advisor* when we were just getting it off the ground. Becky Lenzini and I met with Martin numerous times. Martin was then employed by Choice, and Choice was interested in the fact that *TCA* had reviews of all sorts of electronic products and databases. We even had a big meeting at Fleet Landing Restaurant and Bar at the foot of Charleston's City Market. But the magic of the seafood did not work. We did not sell *TCA* until 2022 when Annual Reviews purchased it, and Martin had moved on.

Shirley Davidson

There is no one, absolutely no one, who deserves more credit for the launching and success of the Charleston Conference than the awesomely incredible Shirley Davidson! Really and truly! I had just gotten the acquisitions librarian job, effectively destroying upward mobility for many library technical assistants. I was the new kid on the library block amid several experienced and senior librarians who were supporting the demise of the current library director. But not to worry. Shirley was there, positive and upbeat through it all.

Recently, Leah Hinds asked Shirley to speak at the Charleston Conference participants' welcome reception. Outgoing and engaging as she is, Shirley brought down the house! Shirley is on one of her hundreds of boat cruises now, but she promises to continue as the Charleston Conference historian when she returns! Hooha!

Mitchell Davis

Mitchell has one of those minds that never rests. He's done so many innovative and creative things it blows your mind. Remember BookSurge, the platform with inventory-free book printing and fulfillment that was purchased by Amazon in 2005 and merged with CreateSpace? It allows authors to publish and distribute their books digitally on the Amazon Kindle store. Another Mitchell brainstorm in the book world is BiblioLabs which was acquired by Lyrasis. BiblioLabs is an innovative Charleston technology and creator of the pioneering BiblioBoard e-book platform.

Richard M. Dougherty

Richard was one of the very first Charleston Conference keynote speakers. He was so famous and well-respected that he added to the positive reputation of the Charleston

Conferences. Richard helped establish the *Journal of Academic Librarianship* and served as the director of libraries at the University of California, Berkeley and the University of Michigan. He was also ALA president 1990–91. At retirement, he started his own consulting firm, Dougherty and Associates.

Bob Dukes

Bob Dukes was a physics and astronomy professor at the College of Charleston. In the 1980s and '90s, when we established departmental book budgets and faculty managers, Bob volunteered and was an early supporter and advocate of the new process. Bob involved me in researching several scholarly papers. When my father-in-law saw the Strauch name on a scholarly paper, he was impressed, and I thanked Bob for the privilege. We have been friends ever since. In 2014, Bob and his wonderful wife, Ann, established a scholarship for physics and astronomy students. In 2018, it was announced as the Bob Dukes Endowed Scholarship!

Barry Fast

Where can I begin? Seems like I have known Barry Fast forever! Before Academic Book Center, Taylor Carlyle— frankly, I can't recall them all! If Barry asks you to lunch or dinner, take him up on it. One thing I can remember is that Barry knows all the very best restaurants anywhere in the world! One Indian restaurant in London had the very best lamb chops I have ever put in my mouth!

Raissa Fomerand

Raissa and the Librarian's Yellow Pages. She had an idea, and it was a good one. But she needed an expensive infrastructure, and she did her best to afford it! Her house was full of computers, printers, fax machines, paper, and she even bought or rented a huge Xerox machine to make copies. She had two young boys and a husband who worked for the UN. After several years, she located a buyer for the LYP. It was on to the next project!

Charles Germain

Charles is one of those men who is irresistible. His blond hair and thick French accent don't hurt, but he is also a smart businessman. Charles left France to relocate in the United States. He started working for Dick Rowe and Faxon before branching out into other ventures. He came to the Charleston Conference often and encouraged me to draw up a business plan for *Against the Grain*. Meanwhile, he was married to more than one woman; not at once, mind you—serially.

Dan Halloran

Dan Halloran was at Academic Book Center when he was offered the presidency of Blackwell's Book Services. Blackwell's later purchased Academic Book Center as was reported in *ATG* in June 1999. OCLC PromptCat was frequently in these conversations.

Chuck Hamaker

If there is anyone in libraries who is a legend, it is Chuck Hamaker! To quote Stephen Rhind-Tutt: "Chuck was just fantastically and beautifully outspoken. Chuck would go on a rant, and he would often have a really good point." I remember attending ALA and a talk by Chuck. It was standing room only. Chuck is a committed and passionate speaker! An inspiration to all of us timid types!

The Hannay Way!

Many of you remember Bill Hannay (1944–2020) fondly from his years of presenting in the Long Arm of the Law panel at the annual Charleston Conference. Bill was a partner at Schiff Hardin LLP in Chicago, IL, who specialized in federal and state antitrust law, intellectual property law, and other trade regulation laws, and was the author or editor of nine books on antitrust and intellectual property law, including *The Corporate Counsel's Guide to Unfair Competition*, published by Thomson Reuter's West Publishing. He presented on legal cases and topics affecting the world of libraries and publishing, and he did so with an ineffable sense of humor and verbal charm. His signature move was to write hilarious original lyrics to a showtune or other familiar piece of music that tied in with his presentation topic, earning him the nickname "The Singing Lawyer" among conference attendees.

It was 1990 when I got a tip about a great lawyer to speak at the Charleston Conference. I had no idea what was in store for the conference and *ATG* long term. Besides writing cases of note and short pieces on legal happenings in the library and publishing world, Bill was quick to research whatever *ATG* asked him about.

Bill connected with Ann Okerson and became a regular speaker at the annual Long Arm of the Law panel on the last day of every annual Charleston Conference. Bill also contributed regular articles for *ATG*'s Legally Speaking column, as well as separate sessions during the conference. He spoke about everything—the market power of publishers, fair use and unpublished material, the right to be forgotten, MOOCs (massive open online courses), the copyright on literary works in electronic databases, and much more!

I could go on and on. The thing that was so very special about Bill was his sense of humor among rather dry subjects. Bill was a playwright, poet, and singer! You can hear him singing in many of these legal episodes. His creativity knew no bounds! Besides several plays that he leaves behind, his wife Donna, his two daughters, and son are also entertainers. We all miss him horribly! There is so much going on now that would benefit from his amazingly serious and yet humorous points of view!

I want to always remember him with a smile, as he would have wanted. When the life of someone who was so very alive ends, we can preserve what little bit remains for posterity. We hope you enjoy this compilation as a memorial to Bill Hannay, "The Singing Lawyer!" https://youtu. be/j_cb8M9Pi2E

Karen Hunter (1945–2018)

Karen Hunter had a remarkable career in scholarly publishing. She joined Elsevier in 1976 and retired as senior VP of global, academic, and customer relations. Despite squabbles in the library community, Karen oversaw many pioneering initiatives like ScienceDirect. She was able to genuinely communicate and negotiate. I was always told she was a librarian, and I believe it. Karen was easy to know; she was down-to-earth and friendly. I invited her to the very first Fiesole Retreat, which she came to with the wonderfully efficient John Tagler. When she asked about accessibility, I assured her it was easy. STUPID ME! It was very difficult to get around in Fiesole! I was just young and uninformed, not to mention stupid, but John and Karen powered through amazingly! There is an annual Karen

Hunter lecture every ALA. Karen had promised to write an article for *ATG* about "what keeps me awake at night," but it was not to be.

October Ivins

Talk about famous! October is it! She started at University of North Carolina-Chapel Hill Library working for Marcia Tuttle. Among other projects, she has worked for Ivins eContent Solutions, where she and Chuck Hamaker started the Charlotte Initiative, which led to a Mellon grant. October and Will and their grandchildren are having a blissful retirement!

Ann Kabler

Ann Kabler has been a wonderful friend through the years, and we still have lunch together as much as we can. When Bruce and I moved to Charleston, the first library I contacted for a job was the Medical University of South Carolina, since I was a certified medical librarian. Ann Kabler was the assistant director. She was very congenial, but there were no professional librarian job openings. So I was on my own. I got two brief jobs with South Carolina Low Country AHEC, setting up libraries in hospitals back in the '70s, when hospital libraries had to be accredited by the Joint Commission on Accreditation of Hospitals.

Hospitals were required to have access to a library. When I got tired of traveling around the state to hospital libraries, I also was hired as head librarian at Trident Technical College. I was lucky to get the acquisitions librarian job at the College of Charleston a year or so later. Whew!

Edna Laughrey

Edna Laughrey approached me about selling ads for *Against the Grain* just after it was launched in 1989. She had retired as a librarian at the University of Michigan and had set up her own company, Laughrey and Associates, representing book publishers. She loved going to all sorts of book-related events, like American Booksellers Association (ABA) Institutes. She was interested and supportive of Bruce's and my writing. I remember her coming back from ABA with a book called *Along Came a Spider* by James Patterson. She had realized that it was a competitor and that I would be interested. Edna continued to sell ads for *ATG* for several years until she decided to retire again.

Becky Lenzini

Becky and I disagree on the first time we met, but I vividly remember Becky speaking at a workshop at UNC-Chapel Hill (we didn't call them webinars back then) when she was working for Faxon. She was a great, enthusiastic speaker, and I invited her to speak at the Charleston Conference more than once. Moving right along, Becky was hired by Ward Shaw and CARL (the Colorado Alliance of Research Libraries) to start and launch the UnCover Company, founded in 1993 as an online article delivery service, table of contents database, and keyword search index. I remember Ward and Becky searching around for a name for the new service. I believe that UnCover was a brilliant choice. It turns out that in August 1995 an agreement was reached for Knight Ridder to acquire a 100% interest in the CARL Corporation.

Tom Leonhardt

Tom was the head of acquisitions—or was it technical services?—at Duke University, where I had been the Duke School of Nursing librarian. When I started the Charleston Conference, I invited Tom and other local librarians (like Bill Schenck, Paul Koda, and John Ryland) to attend the first Charleston Conference. Tom came to the Charleston Conference another year, and he spoke numerous times. He also encouraged others to come to the Charleston Conference, and he continued to come to the Charleston Conference as well. Much later, when I was head of technical services at the Addlestone Library in Charleston, we hired Tom as a consultant to evaluate our College of Charleston book collections.

Mary Ann Liebert

She is a pistol, an incredibly talented woman who knows what she wants and how to do it. When she invited me to her office in Larchmont, NY, I didn't know what to expect. There was an incredible secretary and several editorial assistants. Mary Ann was very much in charge. Over the years, I have heard from Mary Ann by telephone, and she has invited me to her offices several times. Her brain is always working overtime. She even showed me a fiction book she was writing. She had a chauffeur who always picked me up and took me back to the airport. One time, I forgot my pocketbook, and the chauffeur had to take me back to the office to get it. That may have been the last time I visited in person? I wonder why? I think we never had a meeting of the minds. A brief detail: I believe Mary Ann has had two husbands, both with the same first and last name! I told you she knows what she wants.

Clifford Lynch

He is the director of CNI, the Coalition for Networked Information, and a professor at Berkeley's School of Information. I met him when he was working for the Office of the President of the University of California. Cliff has always been an innovator and the first in automation. I wanted to ask him to keynote the Charleston Conference. I was terrified, but did encounter him at an

ALA and asked him. He agreed and has spoken many times in Charleston and Fiesole! He loves to travel on red-eye flights, so you are never confident that he will make his talk, but never fear, he always does! Whew! Maybe he has an AI assistant?

George Machovec

George Machovec, the executive director of the nonprofit Colorado Alliance of Research Libraries, is one of those astutely patient behind-the-scenes guys. He's a great listener and consequently is able to get things done quickly and efficiently. I appreciate that he is enthusiastic and very helpful with applying technology to library services. George helped get *The Charleston Advisor* off the ground, and as *TCA* was being retired to other pastures, he worked to facilitate the publication of the final issue.

Mike Markwith

What a guy! I don't remember when I first met Mike Markwith, but I feel like I have known him forever! I think that Mike started as a sales rep in Charleston and surrounding territories. Mike started working with the Charleston Conference early, really early. In fact, I remember when we used to give gag gifts to Charleston Conference speakers (racy magazines to Sandy Paul, a cactus to Knut Dorn, and many other crazy items!). Mike L was always there to help me go to the Dollar Store or other inexpensive venues and select some of the best gag gifts! It was great fun, but we didn't keep it up—too many speakers and not enough time. But let's not stop here. Mike Markwith is a very serious businessman! I can't remember nearly all the businesses he has been hired by—Blackwell's, Swets, WT Cox, SkyRiver Technologies, TDNet, and more! I was really impressed by his acquisition of Journal Finder, an A–Z link resolver with an ERM component which was developed by Tim Bucknall and UNC-G librarians.

Martin Marlowe

Martin is pretty interestingly awesome! He has two sons who, when they were younger, were learning all about falconry. In his spare time, however, Martin has created Maverick Publishing Specialists, lead analysts on many assignments. He is president and principal. Like awesome!

Corrie Marsh

Boy! It is hard to keep up with the incredibly versatile Corrie! She is now assistant director for operations, Office of Research, Old Dominion University, Hong Kong SAR. Corrie has always made such positive contributions to programming and editing with the Charleston Conference (assuming you can keep up with her!). Maybe we will see her in November? Wonder if she still has her pets?

Audrey Melkin

Audrey has been great fun at all the Charleston Conferences! She loves to dance and sing! I remember her dancing at the No Name Cafe in downtown Charleston! Audrey has always landed on her feet regardless! Audrey is retired after a long, rewarding career! She is continuing with her piano, taking art classes (pastels and stained glass), going to concerts, museums, and galleries, just enjoying life's slower pace. Audrey was always busy and having lots of fun!

Sara Miller McCune

Seems like I have known Sara forever! I first met her outside the Mills House Hotel when Lyman Newlin introduced us. We were having one of the very first Charleston Conferences there. Sara had founded Sage Publishing in 1965 to support the dissemination of usable knowledge and educate a global community. Sage provides international innovative content through its nine hundred journals and over eight hundred books each year in many subject areas. I visited Sara in California several years ago in one of her many residences near Yosemite National Park. It was a delightful visit: we barbecued vegetables on skewers and walked around talking convivially. Sara even offered to let me drive her gorgeous Mercedes more than once. Tempting. But I am not married to a lawyer for nothing!

Bob Miranda

There are a lot of Bob Mirandas, but not the one I am looking for. Here goes what I remember. Back in the 1980s, Bob Miranda worked for Pergamon Press. Among other projects, he oversaw the journal *Library Acquisitions: Practice and Theory.* He loved opera, and a group of us had a scrumptious dinner one evening in New York.

Jim Morrison

Jim was a wonderful sales rep for University Microfilms back when all of us had and needed microfilm! It was a real pleasure when he visited. He and his wife have a great place in North Carolina, and Jim is an encyclopedia about all that was going on back then! We had a great memory phone call just the other day!

Lyman Newlin

Lyman came to one of the first conferences and never stopped coming. He was one of the most energetic, charming, wonderful old men I have ever known. Lyman never ran out of energy or stories. Or beer. He rode the train wherever he went. I'm not sure he could drive. You couldn't start a conversation with him without his mentioning his favorite jobs. His dream job in his youth was at Kroch's and Brentano's, the largest bookstore in Chicago. To him, it was a magic Ali Baba's cavern of knowledge. He then worked for Richard Abel when Dick invented the approval plan. It was a heady time. They felt they had done an early Google-type thing and totally roiled the bookselling market for libraries. They were masters of the library book universe with a big expense account from investors. He introduced me to Richard Abel and John Chambers (Wiley), and we wrote a monograph together. For a time, Lyman wrote a column for *Against the Grain*, "Papa Lyman Remembers." They were always charming and had details of Chicago and the Great Depression. But he never learned to type and would handwrite them on a legal pad, with inserts and arrows and near gibberish that I had to transcribe. Maddening. In his last years, Lyman used a wheelchair, but still rode the train down and motored around the hotel in a mobility scooter.

Jim O'Donnell

Guess I am lucky that Ann and Jim O'Donnell's vignettes are close together! Karma! I met Jim when we were doing an early Penthouse interview of can't recall his name, a wonderful guy who was beginning a promising career at Microsoft. Unfortunately, he and his wife were on vacation in Spain, I believe, when the cab they were traveling in drove off a cliff and they were both killed. A terribly sad ending. Still the Microsoft guy was still alive then, and Jim, the unassuming provost was there, alive, participating in the interview. Jim has a wonderful sense of humor; his BackTalks always bring a smile to my face. Plus, Jim likes to take pictures of each of us with Beanie Babies. Smile.

Ann Okerson

Ann is the very first, most famous Association of Research Libraries type that ever paid attention to me! I met her briefly when she worked for Jerry Alper, when they had a periodical business. Ann has since climbed huge heights. She has worked for the Center for Research Libraries, Yale University, and is now director of the Offline Internet Consortium. Ann is incredibly connected, alert, energetic, involved, and full of ideas. She travels everywhere, domestically and internationally. All my kudos are inadequate because Ann the wonder woman has done and does so much! For the Fiesole Retreats, the Charleston Conferences, *Against the Grain* (don't you love BackTalk?), The Long Arm of the Law—and I can go on and on!

Bill Potter

Bill is fabulous friends with Becky Lenzini and Ward Shaw. Bill is an Illinoisan who grew up in Belleville, near St. Louis. Bill introduced Becky Lenzini to Ward Shaw

when she was working at Faxon. They were both working for Michael Gorman at the University of Illinois. Also,
Bill was at Arizona State University as head of tech ser-
vices reporting to Don Riggs. That's where he encountered
George Machovec. Bill was library dean at the University of
Georgia for twenty-five years! The Charleston Conference
invited him to keynote, which he did masterfully!! But the
Charleston Place bill was definitely as memorable! I remem-
ber reading Bill's fortune from Greek coffee grounds over
dinner one night in Chicago at the Parthenon Restaurant.
(I learned to do this at my loving father's knee ages ago.)
Fun!

Otto Rapp (1919–1991)

He was only about five feet tall, but he packed a mammoth
grey handlebar moustache and could outwalk anybody. It
was also extremely hard to get a Pergamon Press catalog
from him. Growing up in Vienna where his parents owned
a bookshop, Otto had worked with libraries and publishers
since childhood. It's hard to imagine ALA without him. He
retired from Pergamon but was replaced by the wonderful
Inge Valentine.

Lynne Reiner

Lynne has recently been celebrating forty years of independent publishing! LRP is an independent publisher

and distributor of books in Boulder, Colorado. They publish high-quality, cutting-edge scholarly books in politics, social science, and the humanities. I remember Lynne's riveting talk at the Charleston Conference!

Stephen Rhind-Tutt

I have very many—countless—people I have known, but at the very top of my list is Stephen Rhind-Tutt. I remember the very first paper he gave. It was, I believe, around 1986, when Stephen was working for Chadwyck-Healey. His paper was about pricing models and was incredibly accurate and quotable. We talked about it for many subsequent years. Talk about an entrepreneur! Stephen has launched several businesses of his own with several of his colleagues, including the dynamic Eileen Lawrence and others, such as Alexander Street Press and Coherent Digital. Wow! What a businessman!

Digby Sales

One of the perks of the conference organizer lifestyle is you get invited to speak all over the map. My most memorable one was a library conference in Johannesburg and at the University of Cape Town. Jo'burg was a big, filthy city with security guards out in force at the conference hall. English is their lingua franca, so communication was easy. My husband Bruce is a professor and talks for a living, so getting up in front of a crowd was a breeze for him. I'm more self-conscious and need extensive notes.

Of course, when you think Africa, you think wild animals, and we visited a game farm that did cheetah rescue and kept a savage pack of African wild dogs (*Lycaon pictus*), a terrifying sight.

In Cape Town, we stayed in a Dutch-style gabled B and B with Table Mountain and the university looming above us. A very lively American woman ran the uni library and was proud of the "library commons," which was the new buzz at the time. It was nothing more than students socializing rather than being shushed in the traditional mode—the transition of the library from a temple of books to a place to plug in the soon-to-appear iPad.

Digby Sales was one of our hosts and a frequent Charleston Conference attendee. He was a librarian at Cape Town, now retired and living in Vancouver. His grandfather had insisted that a gentleman always wears a jacket both indoors and out, and Digby held to that air of formality. Otherwise, he was full of fun and a delight to be around.

He showed us around Cape Town, the National Botanical Gardens, tea at the Mt. Nelson Hotel. We drove through wine country, visited the library of Stellenbosch University. We rode a tour bus down to the tip of the Cape through pretty towns with aged women lawn bowling, and beaches with high, curling surfing waves. At the end of the line, you walked up a rocky promontory and looked out on a vast ocean with nothing between you and Antarctica. Very lonesome feeling.

It's always a shock to find that the world doesn't have American tort law, and you embrace a lot of risks on your own. The park was teeming with baboons. And right there on the promontory was a snack bar. The human herd exited the bus and moved en masse to stuff their faces without regard to circling predators. Baboons were slinking among parked cars, prancing across car roofs, darting hither and yon with sandwiches and ice cream bars the lure. They have wicked teeth and arms powerful enough to rip your limbs off. Periodically, a man would come out of the snack bar and wave a club and yell at them. Then go back inside. Among the feckless humans was an Italian *pater familias* with children in tow who thought it a hoot to beat his chest like Tarzan and run roaring at the baboons. I kept waiting for him to be savaged, but some higher power was looking out for him.

Della Sar

Della was one of my special most favorite people. She worked over forty years in scientific, technical, and medical publishing, most recently as the marketing and sales director of Nature Publishing Group. She retired to follow her passion—the charity she set up after she was saved from drowning by a fisherman on the beach at Sri Lanka at the time of the Asian tsunami on December 26, 2004, and subsequently witnessed the destruction of lives and homes in Sri Lanka. Della set up this charity with her husband: The Friends of Della and Don.[4]

Bill Schenck

When I first met Bill Schenck, he was working at UNC-Chapel Hill. He was supportive of the Charleston Conference and registered to attend. Bill moved to the Library of Congress. Not sure what's up with him these days. Anyone know?

John Secor (1932–2018)

What a wild man! I remember John wanted to go places and get things done! John had a dynamic personality and was a successful entrepreneur. He had a great love of books and libraries, and in 1971, in the basement of his home in Contoocook, NH, formed Yankee Book Peddler, Inc. He grew YBP to a successful national and international company. He is survived by his wife Sally, nine grandchildren, and three great-grandchildren. In 2015, EBSCO acquired YBP.

Christine Stamison

Christine is one of my favorite Greeks! Not related, but we Greeks hang together. I met Christine's wonderful mother several times, and it was great to know them both.

After working at Swets and Blackwell's, on August 5, 2013 Christine was named by the Center for Research Libraries as the Northeast Research Libraries Consortium (NERL) director. By the way, NERL was founded at Yale by Ann Okerson in 1996 as a consortium of research libraries. Christine retired in January 2022. Small world!

Dan Tonkery (1946–2021)

Dan was born in the coal-mining region in West Virginia and attended the local one-room school. He used a keypunch machine to do inventory, and his summer job was as a Fuller Brush salesman and later the Encyclopedia Britannica. He studied biomedical communications at the University of Illinois and ended up at the National Library of Medicine. Dan has been an administrator at UCLA, Readmore, Faxon, and EBSCO. His final job was president and CEO of Content Strategies. Of course, Dan had many innovative ideas, and he was a first-class learner and innovator. He loved to play golf everywhere and anywhere, and especially to travel! The Fiesole Retreats were always on his itinerary.

Marcia Tuttle

Marcia Tuttle earned a bachelor's degree in religion from Duke University and an MLS from Emory University. She worked at the libraries of Emory University, Princeton University, and the University of Vermont, but the majority of her career was spent at the University of North Carolina at Chapel Hill, where she retired from her position as head of the serials department in 1997. Marcia is most recognized for her contributions to serial work. She published the influential textbook, *Introduction to Serials Management*, in 1983, which was later expanded and reissued as *Managing Serials* in 1996. From 1985 to 1995, she originated and co-edited the series *Advances in Serials Management* with Jean G. Cook. She founded the *Newsletter on Serials Pricing Issues* (*NSPI*) in collaboration with the subcommittee of the Resources and Technical Services Division (RTSD) publisher/vendor library relations committee. Active from 1989 to 2001, the *NSPI* was a pioneering electronic newsletter that covered all aspects of serial librarianship. Tuttle chaired ALA's RTSD (now Association for Library Collections and Technical Services) serial section, and the conference planning committee (CPC) for the North American Serials Interest Group (NASIG). In 1985, she was honored as the first recipient of the Bowker/Ulrich's Serials Librarianship Award for her exceptional work in serials.[5] By the way, October Ivins, who was mentored by Marcia, tells me that Marcia is happily settled in a retirement home with several male admirers!

Anthony Watkinson

Talk about key! The Charleston Conference would not have been successful without the spectacularly awesome

Anthony Watkinson! From nearly the first conference, Anthony filled the roles of moderator, emcee, conversationalist, entertainer, urbane comedian, manager, organizer—whatever was needed. He was our very first recipient of the Vicky Speck Leadership Award! We all love him! Anthony lives in a delightful cottage in Woodstock, Oxfordshire, across from Churchill's graveyard. You can never fail to recognize him with his silver Lytton Strachey beard. His lovely wife Sarah is an equestrienne, poet, and associate provost of an Oxford college. She is a biologist who has written several treatises on fungi and dung beetles while writing fiction including *Photovoltaic: Love Songs to Greenery* and *Native Soil*, a contemporary romance that asks questions about the way we live in the age of mass destruction.

David Worlock

David is a Cambridge history graduate who joined Thomson Reuters as a trainee in 1967. Between 1980 and 1985 he was the CEO of EUROLEX, the UKs first online service for lawyers acquired by Reed Elsevier in 1985. In that year he founded Electronic Publishing Services Ltd., which he sold to Outsell in 2006. David now co-chairs and manages Outsell Executive Programs. David continues to be involved in advisory roles and his interests, like rugby and pig farming.

On one of our more magical occasions, my husband and I met with David at the Reform Club in London. Yes, the club where Phileas Fogg made his wager he could travel around the world in eighty days. And it is a breathtaking Victorian creation. David was living in the small village of Speen and had sold his business to Outsell. He had just completed *Facing Up to Father* (Marble Hill, London, 2020) a memoir of his father's ambitions for his son, and how David had other plans. The book is awesomely charming and wonderful, a record of Cotswolds England in a lost age of the 1930s, '40s, and '50s.[6]

Susan Zappen

Susan came to Skidmore in 1995 as head of Scribner Library technical services. In 2001, she was named associate college librarian for collections. She was president of Eastern New York Association of College and Research Libraries chapter and named librarian of the year in 2006, and went on to encounter the technological revolution. Susan shares my love of horseracing and goes to many events like the Kentucky Derby.

NOTES

Chapter 4

1. Bruce Strauch, and Katina Strauch, "Foreign exchange rates and journal pricing," *Library Acquisitions: Practice & Theory* 13, no. 4 (1989): 417–422, https://doi.org/10.1016/0364-6408(89)90052-5.

2. Carol Pitts Hawks, "Report on the 'Automated Acquistions: Managing Change' Preconference," *Library Acquisitions: Practice & Theory* 12, nos. 3–4 (1988): 387–395, https://doi.org/10.1016/0364-6408(88)90037-3.

Chapter 5

1. Wendi Maloney, "Inquiring Minds: The Unheralded Story of the Card Catalog," Timeless: Stories from the Library of Congress, July 24, 2017, https://blogs.loc.gov/loc/2017/07/inquiring-minds-the-unheralded-story-of-the-card-catalog/.

Chapter 6

1. *Library Acquisitions: Practice & Theory* 15, no. 3 (1991): 257–421, https://www.sciencedirect.com/journal/library-acquisitions-practice-and-theory/vol/15/issue/3.

2. www.fiesoleretreat.org.

3. William Y. Arms, "The 1990s: The Formative Years of Digital Libraries," *Library Hi Tech* 30, no. 4 (2012): 579–591, https://doi.org/10.1108/0737883121 1285068.

4. "ALA Hot Topics," *The Charleston Report* 4, no. 1 (July/August 1999): 1, https://www.charleston-hub.com/wp-content/uploads/2022/06/Chas Rpt-v.4-1.pdf.

5. imls.gov.

Chapter 7

1. gaillardcenter.org/.

2. Mackenzie Smith, "Data Papers in the Network Era," *Proceedings of the Charleston Library Conference 2011*, http://dx.doi.org/10.5703/1288284314871.

3. Lisa Hinchliffe, and Lauren Kosrow, "'Happiness is Library Automation': The Rhetoric of Early Library Automation and the Future of Discovery and Academic Libraries," *Proceedings of the Charleston Library Conference 2014*, http://dx.doi.org/10.5703/1288284315647.

4. Annette Thomas, "The Future of Research Information: Open, Connected, Seamless," *Proceedings of the Charleston Library Conference 2018*, https://doi.org/10.5703/1288284317000.

5. Brewster Kahle, "Building Trust When Truth Fractures," *Proceedings of the Charleston Library Conference 2019*, https://dx.doi.org/10.5703/1288284317192.

Chapter 8

1. Rick Anderson, and Heather Miller, "Let Them Eat... Everything: Embracing the Patron-Driven Future," *Proceedings of the Charleston Library Conference 2010*, http://dx.doi.org/10.5703/1288284314804.

2. Jon Orwant, and Anna Fleming, "Creating a Trillion-Field Catalog: Metadata in Google Books," *Proceedings of the Charleston Library Conference 2010*, http://dx.doi.org/10.5703/1288284314814.

3. Michael Keller, "The Semantic Web for Publishers and Libraries," *Proceedings of the Charleston Library Conference 2010*, http://dx.doi.org/10.5703/1288284314870.

4. Robert Darnton, "The Digital Public Library of America: The Idea and Its Implementation," *Proceedings of the Charleston Library Conference 2011*, http://dx.doi.org/10.5703/1288284314873.

5. Debora Cheney, Chuck Palsho, Chris Cowan, and Frederick Zarndt, "The Future of Online Newspapers," *Proceedings of the Charleston Library Conference 2011*, http://dx.doi.org/10.5703/1288284314878.

6. Ann Okerson, William Hannay, Lauren K. Schoenthaler, and Angela Rathmel, "The Long Arm of the Law," *Proceedings of the Charleston Library Conference 2010*, http://dx.doi.org/10.5703/1288284314816.

7. Annette Thomas, "Our New Job Description," *Proceedings of the Charleston Library Conference 2012*, http://dx.doi.org/10.5703/1288284315072.

8. Anurag Acharya, "Integrating Discovery and Access for Scholarly Articles: Successes and Failures," *Proceedings of the Charleston Library Conference 2012*, http://dx.doi.org/10.5703/1288284315073.

9. Ann Okerson, "SCOAP[3]: Going Live with the Dream," *Proceedings of the Charleston Library Conference 2012*, http://dx.doi.org/10.5703/1288284315080.

Chapter 9

1. Jean Reese, "CD-ROM Technology in Libraries: Implications and Considerations," *The Electronic Library* 8, no. 1 (1990): 26–35, https://doi.org/10.1108/eb044939.

2. National Academies of Sciences, Engineering, and Medicine, "Case Studies on the Introduction of CD-ROM to University Libraries," in *Bridge Builders: African Experiences with Information and Communication Technology* (The National Academies Press, 1996), https://nap.nationalacademies.org/read/5260/chapter/3.

3. Scott Larson, "Introduction and Implementation of CD-ROM Technology in Ohio Law Libraries" (Masters research paper, Kent State University, 1996), https://eric.ed.gov/?id=ED401943.

4. https://sparcopen.org.

5. Lisa Janicke Hinchliffe, "Transformative Agreements: A Primer," The Scholarly Kitchen, April 23, 2019, https://scholarlykitchen.sspnet.org/2019/04/23/transformative-agreements/.

6. librarypublishing.org.

7. Moumita Koley, and Kanchan Lala, "Changing Dynamics of Scholarly Publication: A Perspective Towards Open Access Publishing and the Proposed One Nation, One Subscription Policy of India," *Scientometrics* 127 (2022): 3383–3411, https://doi.org/10.1007/s11192-022-04375-w.

8. Paul Mostert, "TULIP at Elsevier Science," *Library Hi Tech* 13, no. 4 (1995): 25–30, https://doi.org/10.1108/eb047960.

9. Karen Hunter, ed., "TULIP: Final Report" (Elsevier Science, 1997), https://onlinebooks.library.upenn.edu/webbin/book/lookupid?key=olbp12533.

10. Paula J. Hane "RoweCom Files for Bankruptcy, Then Sues Divine for Fraud," Information Today NewsBreaks, February 3, 2003, https://newsbreaks.infotoday.com/NewsBreaks/RoweCom-Files-for-Bankruptcy-Then-Sues-divine-for-Fraud-16764.asp.

11. "Tufts Libraries Suffer from RoweCom Bankruptcy," The Tufts Daily, February 2003, https://www.tuftsdaily.com/article/2003/02/tufts-libraries-suffer-from-rowecom-bankruptcy.

12. Arnita A. Jones, "The AHA and the RoweCom Subscriptions Crisis," *Perspectives on History* 41, no. 5 (2003), https://www.historians.org/perspectives-article/the-aha-and-the-rowecom-subscriptions-crisis-may-2003/.

13. Larra Clark, "ALA Signs Agreement to Mitigate RoweCom Library Losses," American Library Association, March 10, 2003, https://www.ala.org/news/news/pressreleases2003/alasignsagreement.

14. https://scholarlykitchen.sspnet.org.

15. "History of Open Access," Wikipedia, last modified November 14, 2024, https://en.wikipedia.org/w/index.php?title=History_of_open_access&oldid=1257378152.

16. Sibele Fausto, "The Evolution of Open Access: A Brief History," SciELO in Perspective, October 21, 2013, https://blog.scielo.org/en/2013/10/21/the-evolution-of-open-access-a-brief-history/.

17. "A Brief History of Open Access," Open Access 101: Unlocking Knowledge, Blogs.Harvard Network, December 16, 2006, https://archive.blogs.harvard.edu/openaccess101/what-is-open-access/what-is-open-access/.

18. Bo-Christer Björk, "Scholarly Journal Publishing in Transition—from Restricted to Open Access," *Electronic Markets* 27 (2017): 101–109, https://doi.org/10.1007/s12525-017-0249-2.

19. Leigh-Ann Butler et al., "The Oligopoly's Shift to Open Access: How the Big Five Academic Publishers Profit from Article Processing Charges," *Quantitative Science Studies* 4, no. 4 (2023): 778–799, https://doi.org/10.1162/qss_a_00272.

20. Tracy Bergstrom, Oya Y. Rieger, and Roger C. Schonfeld, "The Second Digital Transformation of Scholarly Publishing: Strategic Context and Shared Infrastructure," Ithaka SR, January 29, 2024, https://doi.org/10.18665/sr.320210.

21. Marc Schiltz, "Why Plan S," Plan S, September 4, 2018, https://www.coalition-s.org/why-plan-s/.

22. "Plan S Principles," Plan S, June 11, 2020, https://www.coalition-s.org/plan_s_principles/.

23. "Timeline of Open Research at Springer Nature," Springer Nature, https://www.springernature.com/gp/open-research/about/timeline.

Chapter 10

1. Margalit Fox, "Henriette D. Avram, Modernizer of Libraries, Dies at 86," *New York Times*, May 3, 2006, https://www.nytimes.com/2006/05/03/us/03avram.html.

Part 5

1. fiesoleretreat.org.

2. Joel Silver, "Exit Interview; Jake Chernofsky," *RBM* 1, no. 1 (2000): 77–82, https://doi.org/10.5860/rbm.1.1.182.

3. Here it is! Brian Cox, "The Pergamon Phenomenon 1951–1991: A Memoir of the Maxwell Years," *Logos* 9, no. 3 (1998): 135–140, https://doi.org/10.2959/logo.1998.9.3.135.

4. friendsofdellaanddon.com.

5. The American Library Association Archives, https://archon.library.illinois.edu/ala/?p=creators/creator&id=4191.

6. davidworlock.com.

INDEX

Page numbers in *italics* refer to photographs.